Evelyn,

Thank you for championing the moment.

Onward!

Mike

The Organizational Champion

How to Develop Passionate Change Agents at Every Level

MIKE THOMPSON

New York   Chicago   San Francisco   Lisbon   London
Madrid   Mexico City   Milan   New Delhi   San Juan
Seoul   Singapore   Sydney   Toronto

The *McGraw-Hill* Companies

1 2 3 4 5 6 7 8 9 0 DOC/DOC 0 1 5 4 3 2 1 0 9

ISBN 978-0-07-162486-2
MHID 0-07-162486-4

McGraw-Hill books are available at special quantity discounts to use as premiums and sales promotions, or for use in corporate training programs. To contact a representative, please visit the Contact Us pages at www.mhprofessional.com.

This book is printed on acid-free paper.

To my wife Mel, my champion

And to my kids—Blake, Alex, and Jax—for
teaching me courage and compassion

CONTENTS

CONTENTS

CONTENTS

ACKNOWLEDGMENTS

One of the best things about writing this book is having the opportunity to consider those people who have inspired me. The core inspiration for *The Organizational Champion* came from four people I've never met.

Author Brennan Manning ushered humility into my life through his book *The Ragamuffin Gospel*.

Twentieth century English writer G. K. Chesterton, through his book *Orthodoxy*, helped me realize that the bigger I try to make myself, the smaller God is.

Author Howard Thurman inspired my pursuits through his quote, "Don't ask yourself what the world needs. Ask yourself what makes you come alive and then go do that. Because what the world needs is people who have come alive."

Author Frederick Buechner's influence through his writing helped me align my deep gladness with the world's deep hunger.

Then there are those who have had a direct impact not only on me but also on this book.

My beautiful wife, Mel, was my first, second, and third reader of every sentence, paragraph, and chapter. Even in the late-night hours, she always read my work with a smile on her face. She encouraged me constantly and nurtured me through many months of effort. My kids, Alex and Jax, were considerate with my time, engaging me in play when I needed a break from the project, comforting me in stressful moments, and understanding when I immersed myself in the work.

My work team, the SVI family, is an extraordinary group of champions in whom I have utmost pride. Their creativity and dedication are unmatched by any other team with whom I've been associated.

Autumn Manning, SVI's director of research, who led all research efforts for *The Organizational Champion*, was a constant source of information. Her proactive nature and continuous validation efforts helped confirm *The Organizational Champion*'s concepts and principles. Her work continues as she captures ongoing research from organizational champion behavioral and 360-degree assessments.

Erin Fritsche, SVI's statistical analyst, invested numerous days and nights analyzing data and confirming finding after finding from the massive and complex spreadsheets of information.

Jason Daley, SVI's director of technology, and Brian Newberry, SVI's senior systems engineer, built customized technology solutions that helped create online communities behind the organizational champions concept. These online communities have assisted our research team and have also established a strong network of organizational champions. Check out www.organizationalchampions.com and www.champem.com to get involved in the *champions* conversation.

Tim Harmon, SVI's director of operations, has masterfully aligned our company's products and services behind the organizational champions concept. His work has delivered training solutions, systems, and processes to companies that have enabled them to apply our principles and capture the results.

Murray Williams, SVI's director of media and communications, led the development of the organizational champions brand and its models. Murray's work has also positioned the organizational champions brand well within social media avenues.

Outside of SVI, several organizations, experts, and supporters have made significant contributions to this book. Research partners from CPP, Inc., helped SVI validate its findings with several thousand top executive performers. In the same way, IBM shared research and insights that have helped confirm the principles presented here. Other organizational contributors to the discussion behind the organizational champions principles include Wal-Mart, Tyson Foods, Inc., P&G, VF Corporation, Dillard's, J.B. Hunt, PepsiCo, New Balance, and AOL. SVI's collaborative business partner, Rockfish Interactive, has supported the organizational champions work through the promotion of online and social media communities. John Brown University provided significant support in the research efforts and provided a platform to test and discuss the concepts of the book. Special thanks go to my students Michael Callaway, Abbie Cox, Charles Eckman, Curtis Irby, and Chesney Ward for allowing me to occupy class time with these ideas.

Allyn Elleman and Bob Ford both elevated the quality of the work through their keen and critical eye. I relied on them both significantly for their wisdom. Additional concepts from the book were vetted through Andy Core, who introduced me to the concept of periodization. My own personal sounding board of Aaron Elleman, Rowland McKinney, Todd Bruck, and my sister-in-law, Jayme Thompson, allowed me to debate tirelessly the ideas presented in the book.

My social media friends on Facebook, Twitter, Champ'em, and The Organizational Champions blog—you have been a source of energy through this endeavor because your constant ideas and passions have helped ignite mine.

McGraw-Hill was a consummate publishing partner, as they guided my steps patiently and effectively. The leadership from Herb Schaffner helped ease me into the brand-new world of authorship. Mary Glenn and my editors Knox Huston and Jack Heffron are among the most astute professionals I have ever encountered. I now consider them all special friends.

Finally, to my father, Terry; my mom, Connie; and my brother, Chris, I appreciate the investment you made in me. Through many trials, our family bond remains strong. Thank you for your character and your constant and unconditional love.

INTRODUCTION

Meet Emily.

She's 33 years old and manages a staff of 15 people at a medium-sized company. She's worked there for six years, steadily moving up the ladder to middle management. Her staff meets its prescribed goals, and she has mastered all the standard competencies used to measure leadership. She receives excellent biannual reviews. People like her. They think of her as a good leader.

Truth is, she's not.

When she started working at the company, Emily showed great energy and creativity, pursuing possibilities and driving worthy changes and causes. Over time, however, she got comfortable with the company's traditions and infrastructure. Her growing responsibilities forced her into making safer decisions. Her positive performance reviews convinced her that completing her task list and meeting her deadlines were all the company expected or wanted. And she was right. It wasn't long before Emily coasted comfortably with mediocre results and a secure paycheck. Her company suffered because it was unable to realize new and necessary possibilities, developing instead Emily after Emily after Emily as excellent task managers. Satisfied with the status quo and unable to develop leaders who could push its growth and profitability, the company drifted into irrelevance.

This scenario is all too familiar in business today—at a time when the need for more agile, innovative leadership is greater than ever before. By relying on old philosophies of leadership, companies like Emily's lack the ability to develop and measure leaders who can make a difference—transformational leaders who create positive change, who open eyes and open doors for their companies. I call these transformational leaders *organizational champions*.

This book is about them—and how you can become one.

The Organizational Champion presents a new approach to developing and measuring leadership. In this book, I describe a model that is thriving in some of the world's most agile and successful firms. Executives at these companies have embraced the development of organizational champions as a new cadre of leader who is committed to positive change, to winning in the global marketplace through agility, creativity, and honesty, and to making bold moves that benefit both their companies and the world.

You know many of these companies—companies that demonstrate impressive earnings, growth, and profits in a tumultuous global economy reeling from market shocks. Senior managers at Wal-Mart, Procter & Gamble, IBM, New Balance, Tyson Foods, VF Corporation, and J. B. Hunt, among dozens of other companies, realize that this category of leader is essential in order for them to thrive in today's complex global marketplace. Today's manager and firm face a new set of rules for survival and success.

These challenges include globalization, clashing cultures and diversity, connectivity and communications, corporate scandals, corporate social responsibility, social unrest, environmental and energy crises, challenging economies, aging and growing populations, and the sheer speed at which knowledge whips through the marketplace and around the world. Today's trend is tomorrow's old news.

Who will be the important, successful leaders in this world? Will it be your company? Will it be you? How will you recognize, train, nurture, and manage these leaders?

Crucial questions—and ones I talk about every day. Through SVI, my organizational development company, I speak to corporate and field workers, eager students, self-prescribed leaders, aspiring leaders, and executives almost every day, and every day I hear their ambition for moving beyond old leadership philosophies and worn out leadership programs. Those philosophies simply don't work anymore. The business world needs a new approach that more adequately addresses the challenges in our world today.

That's why I created the core principles for the organizational champion. At SVI, we use this approach to help our clients meet today's unprecedented challenges by focusing on core principles that equip leaders to be more responsive, more creative, and more effective than the rest of the herd. Our system brings new thought, perspective, philosophy, energy, and research to a tired and diluted term—*leadership*.

In *The Organizational Champion* you'll discover the characteristics and attributes that are most critical for the success of an organizational leader who faces the potentially cataclysmic challenges and demands of the twenty-first century. *The Organizational Champion* was written to help people grow and apply these attributes through four core principles:

- Champions are personally grounded and true to themselves—and, therefore, they are genuine and consistent.
- Champions connect with others by pushing aside selfish pursuits for the greater good—and, therefore, they are trusted.
- Champions personally invest, putting themselves on the line—and, therefore, they are inspiring and able to persevere.
- Champions drive transformational change—and, therefore, they succeed beyond others.

We look at champions in today's world and analyze how they created changes that redefined their companies. We work through hands-on exercises that guide you to revelations about your beliefs and passions and about what you can do to become a champion in your own company.

The Organizational Champion will help you break loose from the limitations of outdated leadership models and ignite a new energy toward a purposeful and rewarding life. You'll find new insights into how some of the world's most admired leaders, or champions, have enabled societal movements and corporate transformations, and how companies are succeeding by embracing and unleashing such champions.

Business is the most powerful institution on the planet and is capable of championing global progress through its leaders and their influence. To achieve that progress, however, we need organizational champions.

Creating Champions

For over 20 years, I've pursued the promise of leadership. I've followed the habits, studied the steps, and developed many of the characteristics. I've learned that true leadership requires values, ethics, character, positive habits, action, drive, and results. I've taught leadership at some of the highest levels and been disappointed at what often passes for leadership. I've been both a leader and, at times, a champion. Through it all, I've realized that a gap exists between leaders and champions. I've also realized the potential of business and society through the impact of champions, who make both better.

SVI has invested thousands of hours researching and solidifying the organizational champion's concept, philosophy, and results. We've interviewed hundreds of executives, leaders, managers, and followers to hear their opinions about the short-comings of leadership and their hopes and desires for what a new level of leadership might look like in today's global business environment. We've captured survey data from over 10,000 responders and compared these findings to individual and company performance measures.

Over the past few years, SVI has worked with many of the world's most admired global companies and has tested the organizational champion's philosophies with hundreds of their leaders. Our work continues on a daily basis, but our initial findings show the clear value and benefit of organizational champions and their positive impact on businesses and societies.

Throughout this book, I use our research to support the organizational champion's concepts and applications.

Grasping the Fundamentals

In *The Organizational Champion*, you will master the core principles of an organizational champion, learn a champion's attributes and how you can apply them—the steps you can take to become one. To start you on the way, here's a definition that presents the fundamental concept of an organizational champion:

> Organizational champions are enlightened change makers who are personally committed to mutual values, rather than self-centered ones, and relentlessly driven by possibilities.

Figure I.1 is a model that highlights the definition's core principles and helps to apply the organizational champion's philosophy. At SVI, the measurable impact of an organizational champion is referred to as a champion's echo or *ECChO*.

An echo is a sound reflection. Waves of sound collide with their surroundings and are driven in new directions and repeated. An echo has a lingering effect beyond its origin. Much like that echo, champions' ECChOs should be a reflection of

Figure I.1 A Champion's ECChO

themselves. But it shouldn't end there. Champions should be imitated. Their impact should influence and have a positive and lingering effect on others.

As you view the model, focus first on the *enlightened* section. Enlightenment is all about you, your beliefs, values, abilities, desires, and purpose. An enlightened person is self-realized and authentic.

Counter to the enlightened section of the model, you'll find the *connected* section. If enlightenment is all about you, connectedness is all about you and others—creating a healthy perspective that protects against entirely self-centered pursuits. Connection is established through a champion's personal pursuit toward mutual values.

Just like the *connected* section is a healthy counterbalance to *enlightenment*, a person who is *driven by new opportunities and possibilities*—who pursues bold visions—is also a healthy counter balance to a *change maker* who is fully engaged in executing change. Bold visions must be led by those capable of executing such change. And those who thrive through the change process must have possibilities to pursue.

According to the organizational champion's model, champions are both personally enlightened and attuned to the needs of others. They are visionaries who are driven by the possibilities, and they are also able to execute complex and transformational change efforts within an organization.

Ignite Your Desire and Enable Your Pursuits

To be an organizational champion, you must call upon your emotional energy and connect with a personal sense of purpose. Becoming an organizational champion starts with a deep understanding of who you are at the core—your beliefs about life, your passions, your strengths, and your weaknesses.

From core development, you will gain specific insights into the attributes of an organizational champion and how you can develop and build these attributes within yourself. *The*

Organizational Champion guides you step by step through an empowering process that enables you to:

- Build connection and trust through mutually beneficial initiatives.
- Radiate personal energy.
- Enlist others in transformational change efforts.
- Imagine possibilities.
- Inspire your company's culture.

Improve Your Business

Having mastered the process of becoming an organizational champion, you'll learn how companies can take advantage of these enlightened leaders and how such companies can unleash them to improve the business.

Organizational champions are not a new breed. They already walk among us and have been here throughout history. We've just mislabeled them. By isolating the core principles and developing a new approach, we can recognize and cultivate such champions. With organizational champions, your company will achieve its full potential and maybe even change the world.

PART I

THE PREMISE FOR THE ORGANIZATIONAL CHAMPION

CHAPTER 1

WHAT DISTINGUISHES EXTRAORDINARY LEADERSHIP?

What does *leadership* mean today? It's a term used often, in many contexts, to imply many qualities, that it's tough to say what it means and who truly merits the distinction of being called a leader.

For example, what separates leaders most of us acknowledge as great such as Jack Welch, Mother Teresa, Winston Churchill, John F. Kennedy, Martin Luther King Jr., Mohammad, or Moses from my adventure guide in Costa Rica or from my wife's tennis team captain? They're also considered leaders. I'm a leader, my pastor is a leader, the percussionist at the front of the marching band is too. And my daughter's friend is a leader on the playground.

Everyone, it seems, qualifies.

Are "great" leaders simply known by more people? Are they defined only by their span of influence or the magnitude of their impact? Winston Churchill was a successful politician and military strategist during a time of world crisis. Jorge is a rainforest expert and a conservationist who introduced me to bull sharks and spider monkeys. Both have contributed greatly to our society and to the lives of others. You've likely heard of Winston Churchill. You've likely not heard of Jorge, my Costa Rican guide. They are, in fact, both leaders.

What distinguishes a river guide from a movement maker? What separates the transactional CEO from the midlevel manager who discovers and develops an entirely new market for an old product line? The problem, simply put, is that we no longer know what leadership means. The concept has evolved to exhaustive levels and is applied to any and all situations.

We see leadership in everything—every competency, every project, every relationship. Behind every problem, there seems to be a leadership scapegoat. Leadership has become the abyss of all issues and is used to describe the progress made by any individual. The term continues to evolve in application and dissolve in impact. It no longer distinguishes, and yet we distinguish the term.

The consequence of lacking a clear definition of leadership, of course, is that without one we cannot recognize, train, cultivate, manage, or effectively follow the leaders we desperately need to guide our businesses in the most complex marketplace in world history. Without these leaders, businesses quite simply will fail to meet the unprecedented challenges they face. We need organizational champions to survive and to thrive today and tomorrow.

Leadership Is Baseless

To move successfully into the future of vast complexity and abundant change, we need consistent and core principles exhibited by today's most extraordinary leaders. Without core principles, leadership is baseless.

If someone asked me today, "How do I become a leader?" I would be a fool to try to answer. No single prescription exists. I'd have to ask, "What do you want to lead?" One's circumstance has as much to do with leadership development as any character or skill pursuit. Leadership has no foundation to rest upon. In fact, more than 600 definitions exist for leadership and all of its derivatives. It's hard to agree on a definition, so everyone contributes.

We often define leadership from an existing or anticipated need. The problem is that the needs continue to change and grow—therefore, so does leadership. The solution is not simply to add new aspects to the definition. Instead, we must conceive a whole new way of looking at leadership—through core principles lived out by the organizational champion.

To better understand the need for such principles, let's look at the complex challenges we face today. We're in unique times as businesses are faced with new and enormous economic challenges that have never been experienced before. Consider escalating energy and food costs, plummeting business value, a housing market in crisis, government bailouts, and questionable ethical behavior, and it's no wonder that President Obama's campaign promise for "change" is the forefront communication by successful politicians.

Adding to the complexity is the growing belief that businesses must now address social issues. Today's business leaders understand that their organizations are measured far more than ever before by the impact they have on society. As society changes, businesses must adjust, accommodate, and contribute.

Add to these new concerns the fact that we have as many as five generations working together. Our diverse populations are growing rapidly in all parts of the world with the only exception being Europe in recent years. In just the last 40 years, the earth's population has grown from 3.3 billion to over 6.7 billion. Forecasters predict a population of 9 billion 30 years from now. The number of East Asian workers throughout the world has almost doubled over the past two decades from 660 million in 1980 to over 1 billion in 2004.[1] The number of Latinos has more than doubled in the global workforce, from 124 million workers to almost 250 million in that same time period. The story is similar with Middle Eastern and South Asian workers.

The ease of global travel, our ability to connect across the world within seconds, global business focus and integration, unethical practices, political tension, a rapidly growing middle class, aging populations, economic downturns, and a great deal of social unrest as our planet continues to battle imbalances among societal classes all create a fairly compelling picture that our society is far different today from the way it was in previous generations.

We need capable and trusted leaders to navigate these murky waters, and successful businesspeople know it. Over 75 percent of all CEOs around the world consider leadership development their highest concern.[2] Our postmodern world calls for a postmodern approach to leadership development. We need core principles that keep extraordinary leaders grounded, steady, and equipped to succeed in a world of constant change. Old and evolving leadership models simply cannot handle the myriad circumstances that will now and forever emerge.

In my business career I've been called on to be a leader who energizes a deenergized culture, a leader who brings innovation to a stagnant business, and a leader who builds accountability within an unproductive team. Other leaders face different situations and need to be a different type of leader—a healer, a producer, a networker, an analyzer, a mediator, a visionary.

Therefore, leadership is tied to specific needs that are met through a set of appropriate behaviors and abilities called *competencies*. A healer, for example, would likely need to lead empathetically at times, while a visionary might need to lead through strategy. Empathetic behaviors and strategic abilities are considered competencies.

If business needs are ever-expanding and competencies are developed to meet these needs, then competencies are baseless. If competencies are baseless, then so is leadership as we define it today.

Leadership at Sony is different from leadership at the United Nations, which is different from leadership in Congress, which is different from leadership at the local grocery store. It's different because the needs are different.

If leadership is carried out differently according to given circumstances or situations, then it's not universal. And leadership shouldn't be. Let leadership be what leadership is. It's not a model, but rather a fluid application of behaviors that advances the desired outcome of any situation.

Leadership Is Limitless

Though leadership is not universal, we are making great attempts at creating lots of leadership behaviors. A young growing company might consider the relational behaviors of a leader, while a mature company that is already highly networked might consider the innovative behaviors of a leader. A company in crisis might prize analytical skills, and a company opening new offices internationally might want cross-cultural understanding. But it's all leadership.

As needs continue to expand, so do the leadership behaviors that are required to address these needs. We've aligned social needs with social behaviors, economic challenges with business competencies, and political needs with political skills. So needs and issues determine a company's desired leadership behaviors.

In an attempt to accommodate every business need, leadership has been analyzed and applied thousands of ways. No wonder it's hard to grasp the leadership concept. Leadership has become far too vast. It's been stretched too thin to cover ever-changing pursuits according to the most immediate need or biggest problem.

So far, we've seen that leadership lacks core principles and is deployed according to any number of needs. And we haven't brought in the unique abilities, styles, and desires of each individual in our diverse world into the equation. Instead of targeting a universal model that can be embraced by every individual's style and abilities according to any unique set of business needs, we've tried to make evolving definitions relevant for every individual in every situation. Leadership must now accommodate 600 definitions, continuously evolving needs and adjusted competencies, and it must be embraced by everyone's own unique style and interest.

Impossible.

The playing field must be defined, and leadership philosophy hasn't done that.

We must have a core set of principles lived out by the most extraordinary leaders—champions.

Moving to core principles is similar to a company moving from a policy-driven approach to one that operates on principle. After all, just like there aren't enough policies to accommodate every situation, there aren't enough defined leadership behaviors to accommodate every situation. At some point it becomes unmanageable. We've reached that point in leadership.

The core principles lived out by organizational champions enable them to maneuver through any situation or business need according to their own unique style and abilities. It's not the competencies or behaviors that separate a champion from a leader, it's the core principles. And leaders who live the core principle are more effective and successful than those who do not.

Organizational Champions Are Transformational Leaders

As we move from policy-driven leadership to principle-driven leadership, we move from transactional to transformational leadership. Military leaders, for example, often thrive in transactional, policy-driven leadership. They work by the book, or they don't work at all. On the other hand, combat-tested veterans know that conforming to rules works only up to a point. There always comes a time—often under the most crucial of circumstances—when the rule book no longer applies and what to do next "just ain't written." Of course, knowing when to abandon the book and start improvising is another trick in itself. This is the point at which one moves from transaction to transformation.

My younger brother, Chris, was an F-15E pilot for the Air Force in 2005 and flew missions over Iraq. Most of the time his missions were routine. But on the night of October 9, he and his wingman found themselves at 20,000 feet and low on fuel. My brother, the flight lead, approached the large KC-135 fuel tanker plane and began to fuel his F-15E through the KC-135's fuel boom. Refueling an F-15E takes approximately 12 minutes. At minute number 9, Chris and his wingman received a desperate radio call from a marine ground commander leading a convoy of trucks that was being ambushed. The convoy could not continue to withstand the attack for more than a few more minutes—not enough time to refuel the two planes.

Chris faced a tough decision. Policy dictates that you never leave your wingman. But principle values life. After Chris disconnected from the fuel boom, he left his wingman and flew off to support the marines. He flew in low and fast, while launching his flares to confuse and scare the insurgents, who quickly fled, thus allowing the convoy to recover and get medical attention for the wounded.

Afterward, my brother reunited with his wingman, and they headed back to their base. On the flight back, Chris wondered how he would respond to his commander about breaking policy.

When he dropped off his gear after landing, the marine convoy's commander called to thank him for the maverick decision based on principle rather than policy. He later was surprised by the praise he received in his squadron meeting for making the right decision.

Transactional leaders execute the work, while transformational leaders create a movement through a mission-oriented, principle-based mindset. I'm defining transactions as those standard practices or activities that it takes to execute the work. Clocking in and clocking out are transactional behaviors. So is performing your task list, adhering to standard and timely financial reporting, delivering a typical sales pitch, conducting product quality reviews, or making a purchase. Transactional leaders oversee adherence to process to protect quality and drive efficiency. They coach their staffs to increase proficiency. Transactional leadership is often comfortable, easy, and safe.

I've observed one senior leader who I'll call Dave. He has a team of 100 people, most of them capable of doing their jobs. Dave is a passionate man in his personal life, sensationally committed to his family and to many other things outside of work. He is creative in raising his kids, he makes bold plays in his leisure life, and he serves causes that are important to him. Outside of work, he is a champion. Inside his work he puts on his leadership hat. He becomes a manager trying to accommodate the many requests from this multi-billion-dollar company. He prioritizes his time according to the level of requesters: CEO gets top priority, SVP is next, and a low-level manager need not knock. He has little time for ideas. His output is rarely of his own intention, but rather a deliverable to someone else's request, and his team is frustrated. Résumés are constantly in the works.

Outside of work, Dave prioritizes his time according to the value it brings to his life and the lives of others. He is adventurous and energized. He is a champion at home who settles for the status quo in his career in order to not rock the boat. After all, there's a lot at stake—his retirement, he assumes, is secure.

To many people, he is successful enough. He is a leader. He isn't, however, an organizational champion. And his company suffers because of it. Transactional leadership is important for a business. Carrying out the requirements keeps a business operational. But the ideas, understanding, and anticipations from a transformational leader keep the business relevant both at the present and into the future.

Transformational leadership requires envisioning possibilities that aren't clearly defined. It requires an ability to move beyond what's established to what's possible. Leaders aren't bound by transactions. Many strong leaders are, in fact, transformational. The old leadership philosophy, however, allows transactional behavior without ever demanding the transformational. Our friend Dave, for example, is usually regarded as a good leader by old standards.

Organizational champions don't have such luxury. The transaction is the easy part for them. They are constantly breaking transactional boundaries to transform their businesses into something better.

Even more, our research at SVI suggests that those involved in or leading transformational efforts are more engaged, have a better outlook, and feel more enabled by their organization[3] regardless of their level in the organization.

Organizational Champions Are Trusted

It's hard to top Procter & Gamble as a business partner and client. I've been fortunate to serve P&G through two different companies working in two capacities—first in marketing and now in leadership development. My first experience with P&G came as a result of in-store marketing work through a company I was a partner in called ThompsonMurray. My second opportunity to work with P&G is in leadership development through SVI. Though I worked with different people in different business functions in both of these companies, P&G's expectations and its approach to deploying and enabling both organizations, ThompsonMurray and SVI, were consistent.

P&G is well known for its marketing savvy. It hasn't come close to getting its proper due for developing extraordinary leaders. P&G's leadership development efforts are impressive. P&G knows how to maximize performance by enabling its people and deploying its resources efficiently.

The first lesson I learned in working with P&G is that you'd better be good. You can't fool this company with a savvy sales pitch. Second, you'd better be committed, because the company will stretch you and your organization. Third, you can trust it.

You can trust it because it is committed to mutually beneficial relationships. A win-lose proposition is no proposition for P&G, its employees, its consumers, its communities, or its business partners and suppliers. I've even seen P&G champion win-win scenarios with its fierce competitors to exponentially grow product categories.

P&G has never asked my company to compromise our profits, our values, our work quality, or our people. It is fair (our win), and because of it, it gets our best every time (P&G wins).

This is how organizational champions think. The organizational champion pursues mutual benefit every time. Organizational champions do not manage through intimidation or edict; they build teams by relating through trust and genuine concern, and by communicating frequently and openly.

The old leadership philosophy leaves an open door to self-serving efforts, even, at the extreme, intolerant dictatorships. These self-serving leaders can rapidly gain power and can cause damage that ultimately destroys cultures.

You may have experienced a degree of an intolerant dictatorship through a business partner or someone who works closely with you who pursued win-lose relationships to elevate his or her status while suppressing the status of others. You may have dealt or may be dealing with someone like Joe. Joe was a leader who was smart and showed well. He was admired by his clients and by himself. But his selfish ambitions were exposed, and trust was destroyed with many of his closest allies. Within three years, every member of his core leadership team had left, and even today his leadership team continues to churn. Joe seems incapable of having a mutually beneficial outlook, and therefore, many people don't trust him.

Today, no matter how hard we strive to hide selfish ambition or impure motives, we are easily exposed. The world, and you in it, is much more connected and visible. It's harder to get away with self-serving agendas. People are smarter, knowledge is shared faster, history is readily available, patterns are easily observed, and reputations are developed quickly. Being scrutinized is part of the game, and those who work to destroy are more easily identified and disarmed. Organizational champions are able to keep self-serving agendas in check and embrace mutually beneficial pursuits with others.

The same goes for companies. Many companies are completely captivated by their own self-serving pursuits regardless of the consequences to others. Championship organizations avoid these purely self-serving efforts as well and find greater success in their ability to win in their business and win in society.

In today's business environment, those people and those companies with a propensity to do good and not harm, who have concern beyond themselves, and are socially conscious are building better reputations and stronger brands and are capturing new market share all of which have been previously closed to them. These people and these companies are forming stronger and more trusted relationships with new, influential, and loyal stakeholders.

Organization Champions Can Execute Their Vision

I can think of nothing more dangerous to the health of a business than a transformational, mission-minded leader driving a compelling vision without the ability or propensity to execute that vision. In my organization, we call such leaders *dreamers*.

Ed Zander might be considered by many a dreamer. He was the CEO of Motorola, a Fortune 100 telecommunications company, from 2004 to 2008. Zander had a reputation for being a radical mover and shaker from his previous days at Sun Microsystems. His reputation caught the attention of Motorola, and Motorola's board felt that Zander could provide the appropriate "shot in the arm" that Motorola needed.

For Zander, things started off well in 2004 with the launch of the Razr V3, an ultraslim mobile phone, which was a big hit. It seems that Motorola had embraced the "big hits" model that consumers seem to reward. However, Motorola quickly became a one-hit wonder, failing to develop new and innovative products. Some claim that while Zander embraced bold visions, he was unable to deliver an organization that could execute those visions in a timely manner according to customer expectations.[4] Several product launches were marketed heavily, but the products couldn't get to the stores in time for excited consumers to buy them. Motorola's compelling vision failed to meet consumer expectations in many of its product lines including the Razr and the H5 MiniBlue Bluetooth headset. Hence, over time, Motorola lost its leadership position and is now barely an also-ran, trying to hang on and survive in the telecom industry.

Some consider Zander linear in his leadership. Bold in vision, weak in execution. He failed to develop an operation that could deliver the finished results of that vision in a timely way.

Many leaders suffer similar weaknesses. Conversely, consider the leader who lacks vision but can execute with the best. This type, too, is common in business today. Both types will result in market decline. The leader who can't execute loses because of lost trust with consumers, while the leader who lacks vision loses because of an inability to make a relevant connection with consumers in the first place.

The old leadership philosophy allows for this linear, single-minded approach—visionary or operational. Many of the world's most well-known leaders have built enormous reputations from one fairly linear idea that performed well. Joe Vento, owner of Geno's Steaks in Philadelphia, does one thing, cheesesteaks. He does them so well that his limited menu offering, "cheesesteaks here!" still works after 41 years of doing the same thing.

The formula can be successful and has worked for some for many years. But for every one of these types of leaders who succeeds, there are dozens more who fail to remain relevant because of their inability to envision, adapt, or adjust to demand and change.

Apple was visionary with Steve Jobs, then became operational with John Sculley, then became visionary *and* operational recently with Steve Jobs again.

Leaders can be visionary, operational, strategic, or creative. They can build powerful reputations based on their ability to be amazing in a single area. Organizational champions, again, don't have such luxury. Creating movements and driving organizational transformations demand that an executive, senior leader, or manager think systematically, considering all components of the transformation.

Very few people can be good at all the things that they are called on to be. While few people are both visionary and operational, champions recognize their natural tendency and either compensate by putting more attention to the weaker of their abilities or they recognize and elevate the responsibility of a counterbalance. If they aren't operational, they'll find someone who is and give that person a significant reign. If the champion isn't strategic, creative, or good at communicating, he or she can enable others who are. Organizational champions know where they aren't naturally gifted, and therefore, they know how to deploy others in support of their weaknesses. Through collaboration and shared responsibilities, champions will effectively envision the future and execute within a systems-thinking mindset, considering the whole—all its pieces and their collective impact.

Interestingly enough, there is one qualifier to our research of an organizational champion. While champions don't have to be skilled in all areas to drive transformational change, our research indicates that they must be able to imagine new possibilities. Champions can't assign visionary duty to others. They can't remove "casting vision" from their role or responsibility. Realize, however, that vision for organizational champions doesn't happen within a silo. They seek out help and the involvement of others throughout the vision-forming process. The key is that an organizational champion must be involved in leading the effort. Champions might not be strategic thinkers, but they must be able to envision change. They may not be the best communicators, but they must present a compelling future.

Organizational Champions Don't Let Circumstances Define Results

Leaders are often defined by their leadership or circumstance. A hard beginning might lead to conservative play. Early success might either satisfy leaders or create a greater hunger, thereby altering their organizational plans. Organizational champions, regardless of their situation, take action according to their sense of mission. These champions will overcome a natural propensity to survive through tough times and will follow a higher sense of purpose regardless of the times. They aren't defined by circumstance, but rather by core beliefs, values, and principles. Organizational champions are grounded in principles that are timeless to them and definitely not circumstantial. They aren't easily shaken by the tidal wave of issues or challenges that might come their way. Therefore, they are consistent, steady, and poised. Because they are consistent regardless of circumstance, they are trusted.

These champions do not wait for an opportunity to show their skills. Instead, they create opportunities. The old-model leadership philosophy allows leaders to avoid transformational change if an opportunity simply doesn't present itself. Organizational champions do not get off the hook so easily. They must recognize opportunities where others may not see them. And when they recognize those opportunities they must seize them, mine their full potential, and achieve their goal.

Organizational Champions Use Their Emotions

I'm sure you've heard people say, "Play it close to the vest" or "Check your emotions at the door" in business situations. Leaders are often encouraged to keep their emotions in check, to think logically. It's a standard strategy in a negotiation, not giving the person on the other side of the table too much information to use against you. So, as leaders we wake up on a beautiful morning eager for what life has to present that day, only to intentionally work ourselves into the proper frame of mind—guarded—before we enter our workplace.

Some advantages might be tied to this emotionless approach. We might be better negotiators or critics. We want people to assume that our lack of emotions means that we're steady and unshakable. It's often difficult for us to view an emotional leader in a positive light because we tend to consider only the full throttle of emotions—unbridled anger, melodramatic weeping—of noneffective leaders. But outside of the extremes, our research indicates that a lack of emotions actually depletes the trust others have in us. The most effective leaders give their teams true glimpses of themselves, and they are often vulnerable with their excitement or concerns. A champion's emotional expression is given as a gift to his or her team for the sake of authenticity and energy. Lack of emotion suggests that we have little concern about anything beyond ourselves.

Early in my career, I worked in a very interesting company that was involved in a cultural battle between impassive leaders and those who brought the drama. The culture was highly political and counterproductive to innovation. It kept the organization grounded in a commodity-based business model with tight margins. My boss, Craig, however, was a champion for cultural change, and his passion was highly visible through his emotional energy. Many people in the organization hated him for his leadership style, and they tried to undermine him through corporate policy tricks. Craig was a bad politician. He didn't have time for politics. He was much more concerned with results, and people knew it. He would energetically celebrate the victories but would bring the fire in defeats as well.

Those who worked for him loved him. Many of those who didn't battled his every move. In a few short years, however, Craig was elevated to the C-suite as chief operating officer of this multi-billion-dollar organization largely because he ignited a results-oriented culture through his emotional energy.

Leadership philosophies often ask us to suppress our emotions and play it cool. The champion knows how to use and engage his or her emotions, not suppress them. There are several studies that show how emotions support better decision making, improve performance, and create energy. More on this later. Champions don't have time to play the long drawn out emotional chess match. Rather, you might see them crash the board. Champions don't display unbridled emotions, but they know how to get sensational in order to drive a point and move a team.

Summary

Some of you may be wondering if this theory of organizational champions is yet another innovation, adjustment, or add-on to the already overblown and tired leadership term. I encourage you to keep reading because the principles and ideas presented throughout this book are proven to be timeless and beyond circumstance.

Our world, our society will never go back but will continue forward. Today's challenges will grow grander tomorrow, along with new challenges rising up and adding more complexity. As leaders, as companies, we must learn agility within a commonly shared and core framework. The playing field for exceptional leadership today and tomorrow must be established in order for us to effectively maneuver through the many demands we will face.

Almost every interview and survey we've conducted and conversation we've had during the past three years at SVI has been a journey to establish these core principles for leadership to grow from.

1. *Because we are tested.* Organizational champions must be grounded, self-realized, and enlightened before they can make the biggest impacts through competency or skill.
2. *Because we are a complex planet of diverse people.* Organizational champions must value mutual or global benefit before they can build trust.
3. *Because people are behind progress.* Organizational champions must engage personally and emotionally before they can inspire others to do the same.
4. *Because progress demands change.* Organizational champions must cast a worthy and transformational vision in order for others to embrace change.
5. *Because change is constant and is today's identity.* Organizational champions must enable organizational agility.

CHAPTER 2

YOU NEED CHAMPIONS TO WIN CHAMPIONSHIPS

O ne of my first clients at SVI was a midsized consult-
ing firm made up of 15 very vibrant—as well as some
antagonistic—partners who led a company of over 100 employees. I was brought in by one of the level-headed partners—I'll
call him Sean—with whom I had become personal friends. He
knew that his organization needed a cultural and leadership
rebirth, especially for the business partners. Turnover was ram-
pant, and the threat of a lawsuit was all too common, although
business was steady. I had no idea what I was getting into, but it
wasn't long before I realized that facilitating a growth process
for these leaders would require a significant stretch for me. If
we were successful with this organization, we'd be successful
anywhere.

On a Thursday night, Autumn, SVI's director of research,
and I were invited to our client's partner meeting to propose and
present our development plan of attack. The partner meeting
took place at a plush country club. Autumn and I saw a lot of

drinking and eating and heard casual but sometimes shocking conversations. This group truly lived large. Autumn and I took over the meeting at 7:30 p.m., but 10 minutes into our pitch we had lost all control. The discussion quickly got out of hand. People shouted curse words from all directions, and tempers flared. We were insulted for being such idiots. Though we held our own, Autumn and I finally got to a point at 11:30 p.m. where we realized that a solution was impossible and that we were ill-equipped to guide this team to acceptable results. As we packed up our plans and left the meeting badly bruised, I reflected on one of my first lessons in the people business: never mix cultural or people development presentations with drinks.

On my drive home, my friend Sean called.

"You got the business," he said enthusiastically.

I was so stunned that I immediately accepted the work and told him that we couldn't wait to get started. SVI worked for a year and a half with this company with limited progress. It was a highly political organization full of partners who pursued self-serving agendas and life in the fast lane. Everyone worked exclusively for the paycheck, giving no acknowledgment to an organizational sense of mission. This company had no soul.

It was a talented group, and the members knew their trade and therefore enjoyed a certain level of success—for the moment. But it was easy to see that the success couldn't be sustained. The self-serving culture eventually would destroy itself.

Championship companies elevate beyond short-term success. They don't stop at self-served. They see a worthy mission beyond themselves. They are agile and renewable at precisely the right moments, and they reach new potential time and time again. Because of these qualities, they last. They achieve exponential growth, and they're often industry leaders or in hot pursuit of that position.

IBM is one such championship company, and it walks the talk. But more on IBM's walk later. For now, let's focus on its talk.

Every other year, IBM conducts a global CEO study of organizational leaders around the world of both the public and the private sectors. In 2008, IBM's study included over 1,000 CEOs, general managers, and senior business leaders. The study identified business performers and underperformers based on revenues and profits. The researchers analyzed the characteristics of these companies in order to develop a model of the enterprise of the future—how it would operate to outperform the competition and how it would realize enormous and sustainable success in the future.

Through this study, IBM identified five common traits that enterprises of the future must embrace:[1]

- *Hunger for change.* The enterprise of the future is capable of changing quickly and successfully. Instead of merely responding to trends, it shapes and leads them. Market and industry shifts provide such companies with a chance to move ahead of the competition.
- *Innovate beyond imagination.* The enterprise of the future surpasses the expectations of increasingly demanding customers. Deep collaborative relationships allow it to surprise customers with innovations that make both its customers and its own business more successful.

- *Integrate globally.* The enterprise of the future is integrated to take advantage of today's global economy. Its business is strategically designed to access the best capabilities, knowledge, and assets from wherever they reside in the world and apply them wherever required.
- *Be disruptive.* The enterprise of the future radically challenges its business model, disrupting the basis of competition. It shifts the value proposition, overturns traditional delivery approaches, and, as soon as opportunities arise, reinvents itself and its entire industry.
- *Be genuine, not just generous.* The enterprise of the future isn't just generous and charitable. These companies go beyond compliance in order to fulfill an authentic concern for society in its business actions and direction.

Not only did IBM discover these traits, but these traits were further credited by IBM's own bold moves that helped it recapture a lost leadership position in technology. Like all championship companies, IBM lives these traits in its own business. There are many ways to be successful, but the enterprise of the future will be disproportionately successful for well into the future as it adjusts to opening floodgates of change. Some companies will fail to adjust while others will adjust enough to succeed, but championship companies will embrace these changes to establish long-term advantages.

Interestingly, IBM's study of the enterprise of the future was conducted and introduced at precisely the same time that SVI's research was being conducted on the organizational champion. Our team reached many of the same conclusions by observing and capturing the impact of an organizational champion. Our "eureka" moment came when we realized that these championship companies (or enterprises of the future) depended on organizational champions who are driving global visions, creating agile cultures for change, and making bold and disruptive plays.

While companies in pursuit of championships are authentic or genuine, hungry for change, innovative, integrated globally, and disruptive, they achieve these qualities through organizational champions who enable their companies to win championships.

Enlightened leaders are authentic and genuine. These leaders know who they are at their core and express that knowledge in everything they do. Those leaders who push aside their selfish pursuits for the sake of the win-win scenario pursue global benefit and value. Global integration requires global collaboration. Global collaboration requires trusted motives that are born of mutual concern. Change makers are obviously hungry for change. But what may not be so obvious is that today's change-drivers for global companies are systems thinkers. They drive change across the organization, enabling and involving all stakeholders across all boundaries while considering the system as a whole. They are personally committed as their emotional energy and passion present the seriousness of and elevate the drive for change in pursuit of new opportunities.

Building a championship company is a long-term process. It must be a constant pursuit. Companies are at different stages of their championship pursuits. Some of them have just begun their pursuit, while others are trying to sustain the position. Because companies are at various stages in their pursuit, organizational champions aren't just found in those companies that hold the top spots in their industries. Many of these champions work in struggling companies and are involved in worthy turnaround efforts. The company position is not as important to the champion as the company pursuit of a championship vision.

There is a definite progression toward winning a championship for companies, but champions are present regardless. Therefore, we look at three companies that are each at different stages in their pursuit of becoming championship organizations or sustaining their championship position.

AOL is a well-known global Internet services and media company that has come upon tough times. This company is just now figuring out a relevant business model for today's marketplace and in pursuit of becoming a championship company.

Tyson is a successful organization that leads its industry and is used to winning. But recent challenges have placed new pressure on this protein marketer and its industry. Therefore, Tyson is making bold moves toward securing the top spot in its industry for well into the future.

IBM recaptured its leadership position in the technology world several years ago through its new emphasis on technology services. Now this company is sensational in bringing consistent value to its clients through innovation and integration in order to sustain its success.

In addition to these three companies, we also look at the organizational champions within each of them and examine how these champions are helping to lead the progress. As we discuss these companies and their organizational champions, look for ways to apply their example to your own situation.

A Champion's Impact on AOL's Turnaround Effort

For several years, AOL has been under significant scrutiny, and rightly so. As one of the first out-of-the-gate online service provider companies, AOL dominated the Internet market in the late 1990s and early 2000s. At one point it served over 30 million online dial-up members across several continents. Who can forget the enticing sound of, "You've got mail"? AOL, however, was riding a dinosaur because its primary dial-up Internet service began losing ground to broadband. Unable to quickly adjust its course and shift its model, the company lost relevancy with its customer base. Internal debates about what course to take led to many desperate reactionary moves. AOL lost its focus: What is it—a dial-up service provider, a broadband player, or a content/ad-based business?

The results of AOL's decline thus far have been a workforce reduction of 56 percent and a drop in value from $240 billion to around $20 billion. The offices and hallways of its Dulles, Virginia, headquarters exude a feeling of accepted uncertainty and even doom.

Until you reach the fifth floor.

This is Kim Partoll's realm. She is the executive vice president of Access, business intelligence and new ventures for AOL. In the summer of 2006, AOL officially shifted its focus to a Web ad business model. AOL completely harvested its dial-up business, called Access, grabbing every ounce of value it had, but planting no new seed. The old dial-up model was now going to fund the new Web ad model, which was the entire focus. Dial-up for AOL wasn't going to experience "death by a thousand paper cuts" as Kim describes it. The core product that launched the company's success would be eliminated. That's Kim's job—to milk the revenues out of a dying dial-up business to fund the new ad business model.

Even during such tough times, Kim and her team possess powerful, positive energy. The business doesn't drive the vibe; Kim does. The vibe exists because Kim is an organizational champion. She is not only a key leader in a tough business, but she's leading the charge of the dinosaur. Kim is leading a dying business unit. No such vibe should exist. But get this. Even though Access is intentionally experiencing decline, its profit margins have grown from 47 percent in 2006 to 87 percent in 2008. Access is generating over 85 percent of AOL's cash flow.

The performance improvement from 2006 to 2008 was somewhat preceded and then paralleled by a cultural improvement under Kim's leadership that began in 2005. This dying business segment of utmost importance to AOL's future shows the highest employee satisfaction in the company. Kim's team of approximately 200 has the most fun, is the most engaged, works the most collaboratively, and is more performance-driven than other teams at AOL, according to company surveys.

Champions like Kim love, embrace, and even enjoy such challenges. She has developed a healthy culture and has improved business performance by attacking the challenges head on, rather than avoiding or suppressing them. Her positive energy is contagious, but she's also brutally honest about the business. Though she doesn't play, the electric guitar in the corner of her office seems to characterize her well. She's tough and agile, able to make tough calls while maintaining her compassion and her appreciation of the human spirit.

Kim is a connector, and she champions much of AOL's culture. She has no time for politicking, but rather reaches all levels of the organization, breaking down barriers, healing resentment, and helping people understand where they fit or why there's no place for them to fit at all. As Kim and I talked, she discussed what she views as the keys for championing an organization in crisis.

Allow for Some Dancing during Tough Times

Kim claims that there is a time to dance and a time to march. In her mind, corporations don't do enough dancing, meaning that there's not enough two-way conversations and open dialogue. Dancing allows for debate at and between all levels, which has led to a greater sense of cooperation at AOL. Through "dancing," Kim has built trust and connectivity within a tough cultural environment. She didn't always have good news when she met with people whose jobs were being changed or terminated, but she never rushed through tough conversations or left people wondering. She remained 100 percent present in every conversation, doing a great deal of listening. She could have given a "party-line" answer to tough issues. That would have been safer and acceptable. But it would have also destroyed trust, a desperately needed quality at AOL.

Prioritize and Simplify

Though it sounds easy, Kim demands that her people understand how to say no. You can imagine that a 56 percent reduction in the workforce while milking a dying dial-up business and starting a new business model will stretch capacity. Therefore, Kim's team had to decide what it was going to do, and just as importantly what it wasn't going to do, and where it was going to focus. The outcome of this process of prioritizing and simplifying helped the remaining workforce focus on only those things that were going to drive the business.

Understand Role and Impact

Kim gets involved with people. She invests time in understanding their interests and their aspirations. She knows their strengths, their weaknesses, and their challenges. She also knows the needs of her organization. Through all of this knowledge she is able to facilitate a connection between the strength of her employees and the needs of the organization. She helps facilitate productive restructuring. When Kim facilitates alignment between the individual and the organization, she constantly communicates the impact and results of the positional adjustment or move. All of Kim's employees, therefore, know their relevancy and role, and their fit ignites their engagement even in tough times of change.

Kim is quick to point out that the right strategy carries 25 percent of the weight for any recovery, while culture carries 75 percent. According to Kim, most of AOL lives the cultural keys expressed above very well. Because of this, even though AOL still significantly trails its rivals Yahoo! and Google, Kim has confidence in the future of AOL as a thriving company and a leader in the Web ad business. She believes in AOL's strategy and culture.

A Champion's Impact in the Midst of Tyson's Perfect Storm

Tyson is the world's largest marketer of protein and a company battling the perfect storm. As a large global employer and an industry leader, Tyson is constantly under the microscope of several nongovernmental agencies and watchdog groups. Needless to say, it's in Tyson's best interests to create formal processes and infrastructures that help maintain its quality standards and protect against any tampering. The organization itself demands sound operational structure and quality controls, and this company is led by organizational champions.

Several of Tyson's executives invest significant time in identifying these champions, and once they are identified, these executives take a personal interest in them and prioritize the relationship over other relationships. Following a formalized "champions" development process, these extraordinary leaders are unleashed through stretch assignments for exponential impact. Tyson has to unleash them. The business is too complex and moves too fast for transactional leaders.

Tyson's international president, Rick Greubel, explains the complexity through three cataclysmic events that brought about the call for champions at Tyson. According to Greubel, the first event took place in 2003 when one cow with mad cow disease was imported from Canada to the United States. The global consequences were staggering. This one cow shut down every export market to the United States, and all beef was turned away, which led to a vast oversupply of beef and a drastic drop in prices domestically. The closed export markets and the reduced domestic prices cost Tyson alone over $1 billion in sales.

In 2008, Korea, which had been the second largest importer of beef from the United States, finally allowed U.S. beef into the country. Japan still doesn't allow in U.S. beef, though there is hope that Japan will remove the ban in 2009.

The second cataclysmic event for Tyson and its industry occurred in 2006. Media outlets throughout the world reported avian influenza, also known as bird flu. The bird flu was found primarily in chickens, and from the media reports a panic throughout the world set in as people immediately began avoiding any contact with chickens, dead or alive. In fact, 2,000 KFC restaurants in China stopped selling chicken altogether.

Since 2003, 264 people have died from bird flu.[2] These people either lived or worked with chickens and had direct contact with them. There are some crazy but documented stories of a few people in Thailand who participated in cockfighting events and tried to revive their birds after a fight by giving them mouth-to-mouth resuscitation. Some of these people died as a result of their efforts.

Because of the panic, there was a significant decrease in the demand for chicken around the world. Volumes were down, prices dropped, and the poultry market crashed. To put this in perspective, the Centers for Disease Control and Prevention (CDC) estimates that approximately 36,000 people die each year from the flu (nonavian) in the United States. With fewer than 300 human bird flu deaths over the last five years, society's response doesn't seem appropriate. I don't mean to minimize the impact of the avian flu. The point is that extreme situations, legitimate or not, exist today for our businesses.

The third cataclysmic event for Tyson and its industry happened when grain costs escalated. For 30 years, corn traded at between $2 and $3 a bushel. In June 2008, a bushel of corn rose to over $7. Corn is the highest cost in producing a chicken. Add to the escalating grain costs the significant rise in energy costs, and it's easy to see how the costs for producing chicken meat has increased by more than 50 percent within the last two years. The poultry industry historically makes approximately $2 billion to $2.5 billion in profits each year. These increases in production costs have added over $1 billion in costs to Tyson alone.

Obviously these cataclysmic events have presented enormous challenges to Tyson's business and to the protein industries. Because of these issues and because of the makeup of the industry, margins are tight. No one would blame Tyson for exuding its gravitational force by keeping a close rein on its business and playing it safe in order to get through such challenges.

But Tyson is a gravity-busting company. Rather than playing it safe, Tyson has unleashed its organizational champions to pioneer new ideas and pursue new opportunities. This effort to create a culture that eliminates fear and allows team members to take smart risks and pioneer worthy efforts is paying off.

Jean Beach, head of Tyson's commodities trading and risk management is one of Tyson's champions. Beach brought the first formal commodities trading expertise to the industry to revolutionize how Tyson mitigates risk. The hope is that by participating more actively in the commodities markets and establishing future trading positions in the markets, Tyson will offset volatility and hedge against loss. Through this practice,

Tyson can be aggressive and intentional about avoiding price swings in grain and energy costs.

Beach's leadership brought a number of the smartest commodities traders from the big cities to Tyson's small-town headquarters. Her efforts have helped Tyson effectively maneuver through the erratic price fluctuations of grain and energy—at times saving Tyson hundreds of millions of dollars.

Donnie Smith currently leads Tyson's consumer products division. Smith is a cultural champion at Tyson. He won't call himself the smartest man or the most technically savvy, but he has been assigned to much of Tyson's most visible work and has led some of Tyson's largest divisions. He is a "go to" guy who knows how to engage and lead people and ignite a high performance culture. You'll often find Smith on the stage in meetings or conferences passionately communicating a new leadership model that supports innovation through collaboration, diversity of thought, and dialogue throughout all levels of Tyson. But you'll also see him investing disproportionately in individuals in one-on-one meetings as Smith is a highly pursued mentor for many.

Tyson offers another interesting champion story in Jeff Webster. Webster is Tyson's senior vice president of renewable products, a position that didn't even exist at Tyson before Jeff asked for it. Typical of a champion, Jeff didn't wait to be called. He was involved in many discussions with other Tyson team members about Tyson's potential involvement in energy-producing innovations, and he stepped forward. Because of Tyson's commitment to creating and sustaining an innovative culture, Tyson's previous CEO, Richard Bond, turned Webster loose to develop and refine the concept of converting by-products to bioproducts. Bond asked only that there be no environmental messes and no new costs to the company. Jeff's efforts were going to have to be clean and entrepreneurial.

He formed the renewable products team from a diverse group of people who embraced various opinions and insights and made various contributions. Everyone counted on Jeff's team, and every idea mattered. Using only the resources that currently existed, the team started by asking the "why" and "what if" questions. Team members were free to wonder, to ideate, to test hypotheses, and to fail. Jeff's team was diverse in experience, thought, and makeup.

The team soon discovered that while Tyson maximized the use of the chicken, using the whole bird, front and back, there was an opportunity to turn the chicken's internal organs into higher margin by-products. Webster knew that, though biodiesels are typically made from vegetable oils and not the animal fat that Tyson produces, Tyson could figure out the way to turn it into liquid fuel to power everything from cars to jets. Tyson saw renewable diesel as its chance to cash in on the alternative-fuel boom.

Jeff envisioned enormous revenue streams from by-products that could be created from these wasted guts. Hence, the rallying cry for Jeff's new team became, "No guts, no glory." And it has worked. The move has paved the way for great participation of fats and oils in renewable fuels and has changed the way protein companies can participate in the biofuel industry. According to an article in *Meat & Poultry* magazine in early 2007, "This puts the industry front and center in renewable fuels. This is a huge win for animal agriculture, a huge win for the environment, a huge win for renewable energy, and a great day for Tyson."[3]

Because of this pioneering and visionary work, the renewable products team of 900 people has become the driving force behind one of the company's cornerstone corporate strategies. In just two years it has opened up entirely new markets and delivered significant revenues.

So in 2007, the renewable products team focused on the fat of the chicken, beef tallow, pork lard, cooking oil, and restaurant grease. Its idea was to make all of these significant and renewable sources of fuel; it began to put its ideas into action. Tyson produces 20,000 barrels of fat every day. That's a lot of fat, and it's enough to get oil companies to consider this new source of potential energy. It wasn't long before Tyson established a new partnering relationship with a biofuels technology organization called Syntroleum Corporation.

The new partnership between the two organizations formed a company called Dynamic Fuels. Dynamic Fuels and its technology can process the dirtiest, low-quality and less expensive fats and convert them into a very high-grade synthetic fuel for military and commercial airplanes. Dynamic Fuels plans to make fuel by using all fat and no petroleum.

Jeff's team was released to find new worlds of opportunity, and it has delivered, discovering breakthrough ideas that are ushering in game-changing opportunities for an industry that desperately needs them. Even more, this gravity-busting team's ideas have achieved record profits through four straight quarters, and profits for this group have grown by 40 percent or more each year.

A Champion's Impact on Protecting IBM's Turf

Earlier in this chapter we looked at IBM's study that emphasized the importance of being hungry for change, innovative
beyond imagination, globally integrated, disruptive by nature,
and genuine. Now let's see how IBM walks the talk. Throughout its history, IBM has built a reputation of being able to
reinvent itself to remain relevant. It successfully transitioned
from business machines and typewriters to mainframes, from
mainframes to PCs, and from PCs to business solutions and
services. However, from the mid-1980s to the early 1990s IBM
struggled to find a new identity. It had lost its soul, according
to Lou Gerstner, IBM's CEO from 1993 to 2002. Just prior to
Lou's involvement, IBM was on the brink of extinction. Its market share had crumbled, its cash position was abysmal, and its
products were quickly becoming irrelevant. The world's largest
computer company was in big trouble.

Saving IBM was going to have to happen quickly if it was
going to happen at all, and radical moves were needed immediately. Jim Burke, an IBM board member and the past CEO of
Johnson & Johnson, led the board committee responsible for
bringing in a new leader for IBM. He went straight to Lou
Gerstner, who was the CEO of RJR Nabisco at the time.
Gerstner declined the offer. He knew his abilities, and technological acumen wasn't one of them. He felt that technological
acumen was necessary to run a technology company. Over time,
however, Burke convinced Gerstner that IBM needed a change
agent to lead it, not a technologist.

When Lou took the reins in 1993, he quickly discovered
not only a bleak business and financial position, but a stagnant

49

culture as well. At all levels within the organization he saw fear, uncertainty, and an extraordinary preoccupation with internal processes. He rarely heard mention of culture, leadership, teamwork, or customers[4] in his one-on-one and group discussions. Customers, culture, and leadership didn't seem to matter to the employees, but Lou found them to be his toughest challenges. All lines of the business were down with the exception of a relatively small segment of the business called *services*.

Lou began logging some major air miles as he met with IBMers around the world, listening to their strategies, evaluating their strengths, and posing critical questions. He wanted to understand his company. One thing he quickly learned was that his company didn't understand its customers. IBM was losing their trust. He immediately launched initiatives that put the customers in charge of IBM's future directions. IBM was going to be customer-centric.

Lou continued his radical moves and dismantled an entrenched management committee. He shook up the culture by breaking down fiefdoms and by creating a new board of directors with no IBM insiders other than himself. He continued with changes to the brand and restructured compensation to reflect performance. He put the previous business strategies to break up the company on hold and became committed instead to increasing IBM's value by capitalizing on all of its resources. Lou, it seemed, changed everything and touched everyone in IBM. In less than a year he stabilized the organization. His efforts were truly spectacular.

But now that IBM was stable, the question became, where would IBM go? What would IBM's vision be going forward? Lou had fallen in love with IBM and gained new passion for its potential. He wanted IBM to be number one again, and he established a new vision for accomplishing it. In his book *Who Says Elephants Can't Dance?* Lou explained his vision:

> At a higher level, we had articulated and then led the future direction of the industry—a future in which business and technology would not be separate tracks but intertwined; and a future in which the industry—in a remarkable about-face—would be driven by services, rather than hardware or software products.

Lou was about to bet on "e-business," and services moved front and center for IBM. By March 2002, his vision became reality. IBM was a championship company again, back on top.

What was it about Lou that gave him the edge to pull off such an enormous challenge?

He was truly a champion who found a deep love and passion for IBM, and his work became personal. He made bold and disruptive plays that were game-changers in the industry. But he also realized something that other organizational champions realize: culture isn't one aspect of the game—it *is* the game. More than any other accomplishment, Lou created an agile culture at IBM and, therefore, an agile company that could adjust quickly to constant change and even self-renewal without breaking its core tenets.

Summary

Each of the examples of champions in companies such as AOL, Tyson, and IBM demonstrate the significance and impact of a champion's work through champion characteristics. Kim, Jean, Donnie, Jeff, and Lou—the only CEO in the bunch—are all self-aware and self-realized, confident in who they are. They are all change agents who create agile cultures and, therefore, agile companies. They work beyond their own self-serving agenda and have an enormous passion for their business and their people. Finally, they all describe a compelling future of possibilities, and they are relentless in their pursuits regardless of the stage of their business. Though they all have their own strengths, abilities, styles, and interests, they are each champions at their core.

But champion pursuits aren't just limited to the top leaders in these organizations. I could feature dozen's of stories of field workers and midlevel managers who are champions. You'll read later championship stories about Wal-Mart store manager Jessica Lewis and about my good friend, Seth. But I'll also present how many of the younger generations of workers, those just starting their careers, have already embraced many of these championship principles.

Are you a champion? Are you championing your company or your team toward a championship—building culture and driving transformation?

The next several chapters present the journey to becoming an organizational champion and will answer the questions of how you can establish its foundational traits in your life and for your company.

PART II

BECOMING AN ORGANIZATIONAL CHAMPION

CHAPTER 3

DISCOVER YOURSELF

F rom my perspective, it's hard to top Meg Ryan—beautiful, classy, sensitive, and extremely talented. When I was in college, I actually wrote her a letter inviting her to homecoming. I didn't get a response and didn't expect one. And I'm still a big fan.

I became an even bigger fan after watching her play several characters in one of my favorite movies, *Joe Versus the Volcano*. In the movie, one of her characters, Patricia Graynamore, delivers a profound statement on enlightenment: "My father says almost the whole world is asleep. Everybody you know, everybody you see, everybody you talk to. He says only a few people are awake. And they live in a state of constant, total amazement."

That's enlightenment.

Enlightenment is a crucial aspect of an organizational champion, and we focus on it in this chapter. Many leaders are "asleep," tending to the status quo as their companies slowly fall behind the competition. They lead without insight or passion. In many cases, they don't really know their passions or have long ago traded them in for a safe, comfortable existence.

Organizational champions are enlightened. They are awake to possibilities, seeing opportunities because their eyes are open. They are, to use a psychological term, self-actualized, which refers to the desire to achieve your full potential. It sits at the top of Abraham Maslow's famous hierarchy of needs. Maslow defined it as "the desire to become . . . everything one is capable of becoming."

Our goal, then for enlightenment, is to discover what we are capable of becoming—to be, as Patricia Graynamore tells us, "awake"—and then to muster the courage and energy to achieve our own potential.

I know it may sound strange to discuss abstract concepts like enlightenment and self-discovery and self-actualization in the context of building business leaders, but bear with me. These terms lie at the center of my purpose in this book—creating core principles for leadership so that leaders can confront the challenges of the unprecedented times in which we live.

And now, as the TV announcers say, back to our movie. In *Joe Versus the Volcano,* Meg costarred with Tom Hanks, who plays Joe, a hypochondriac with a miserable job working in the basement of the dismal American Panascope Company. Joe had no passion, no fortune, no family, no friends, no prospects, and no future. And ironically, he has no reason to live until he finds out he is dying. Then he finds every reason to live. His life, overnight, becomes an adventure.

Toward the end of the movie, Joe, barely alive and stranded in the middle of the ocean, floats on a makeshift raft at the darkest time of the night. As he prepares to die, the fullest and brightest moon ascends from the horizon. In spite of his hopeless end, Joe somehow finds enough energy to stand on his weak and wobbly legs and acknowledge the magnificence of the moon. With his arms raised, his silhouette consumed by the moon's bright glow, Joe whispers, "God, whose name I do not know, thank you for my life." At that point and for the first time, Joe discovers himself.

The road to enlightenment begins with self-discovery. And the road to self-discovery isn't always easy. In fact, many people find it a very difficult trek. But by accepting the difficulty—even embracing it—we discover ourselves, and through that discovery we can enlarge ourselves.

An important step on the road to self-discovery is getting past our egos, which can convince us that life owes us a smooth ride. We are always waiting for something better, only to realize at inopportune times how good we actually have it if we would just choose life in all its abundance and with all its tragedy regardless of circumstances.

As we discuss in Chapter 1, champions aren't defined by circumstance. Too often people are defined by the catastrophic or by the great reward. You hear countless stories of how tragic experiences have led a person to a state of depression or addiction. They are unable to recover emotionally from a severe car accident, a bad breakup, the loss of a job, or the loss of a close friend or family member.

Champions, however, learn from such setbacks and through their new understanding are able to recover—and are stronger as a result. They are enlightened through perspective and self-actualization, understanding better than ever who they are and what they are capable of. You might say that they are comfortable in their own skin and are, therefore, confident in sharing *who* they are—their beliefs, values, strengths, and passions—with others. In fact, SVI's research shows that champions are more transparent and do a much better job of showing their teams what they truly stand for, and they lead from this platform. Our research also shows that champions acknowledge their weaknesses, being honest with themselves and others. We know this is imperative because those leaders who fail to acknowledge and share their weakness fail to establish needed trust.[1]

Organizational Champions Have Perspective

I am not an astronomer, even by hobby. But the topic fascinates me nonetheless. Like Joe in the movie, who among us hasn't stood in amazement under a clear night sky? Yet that clear sky, majestic as it is, tells less than a billionth of the story. It can be mind-boggling to think about the vast size of our universe. Amazingly, we don't even know how big our universe is. We've never seen the end and likely never will. In 1990 the Hubble satellite was launched to provide clear pictures of our universe. A discovery satellite orbiting 360 miles above the earth, Hubble gives us astonishing photos and a better understanding of our universe.

Hubble has allowed us to see 10 billion light-years away through its amazing lenses. To comprehend the distance, take 10 billion light-years and multiply it times 6 trillion miles. Are you ready for the number? 60,000,000,000,000,000,000,000 (60 sextillion) miles.

Through Hubble's photos we have discovered hundreds of billions of stars and a few hundred billion galaxies—and counting. Our earth is one planet inside of one solar system within one galaxy surrounded by a few hundred billion galaxies. What does this say about us?

It says that we're not that big of a deal.

Champions not only realize this fact, but they are extremely comfortable with the thought. Through this perspective, they are grounded with a strong sense of self and exude a humble confidence. Champions don't have to be big in the story, but the story has to be big. They know what's important. Even in a massive universe, champions understand the value of every individual, every encounter, and every opportunity. At the same time, they realize that, despite their success, they are a very tiny part of a gigantic universe. They keep themselves in perspective. What matters to champions is not their impact on the history of the universe, but rather, their impact on those people they know and love.

Organizational Champions Are Self-Realized

San Antonio is no place to be in the summer, but that's where I found myself in July 1990 as I entered into Air Force basic training. But worse than the heat—far worse—was Sergeant Madrid, our basic training instructor. He should have been called Sergeant Ma-*dread*. He was the meanest human being I've ever met.

For some reason, Sergeant Ma-dread focused a lot of his attention on me. He made sure that I was the last asleep and the first awake of our flight crew of more than 20 men. That meant three hours of sleep a night, tops. Ma-dread had two methods of waking me up. Some mornings at 4 a.m., he'd creep up to my bed, grab the bed frame, and yank it with all his might, throwing me across the barracks and waking up everyone else in the process. That was by far my preferred method of the two. On other mornings he woke me by lifting me up by my ear until I was eye level with his 5-foot 8-inch smirk.

"Thompson!" he'd yell. "Welcome to another day of testing your mettle." Ma-dread, and through him the air force, wanted to know what I was made of, how far I could be pushed—my breaking point. He may have wanted to know whether or not I had the guts to stand up to him when he went too far.

Though I'd never want to relive it, the experience taught me a lot about myself. It was an opportunity for self-discovery, to "test my mettle," as the sergeant used to say, and find out about my abilities under pressure. Basic training is loaded with contradictions. On one hand, it's about creating a culture of absolute obedience to authority and a culture of conformity. On the other hand, it's about identifying and equipping the mavericks that in many cases will make the best leaders under fire—who will make the right decisions when policy falls short. These mavericks aren't afraid to move and will improvise in uncharted territory.

The twenty-first century presents an abundance of pressure, contradiction, and uncharted territory for leaders. Today, leaders are faced with economic pressures that have only once been greater—during the Great Depression. The financials of businesses today are stretched to the extreme, and no one seems comfortable. Almost every day brings new economic uncertainty, from low consumer confidence and record-breaking home foreclosures to growing unemployment and a crumbling stock market. The strongest financial institutions suddenly disappear overnight. Additionally, the speed of business—of innovation, of the transaction, of knowledge—is at an all-time high. The complexities support the creation and elevation of organizational barriers such as corporate silos interrupting collaboration, unmanageable schedules, and misaligned direction, measures, and rewards.[2] Today, leaders are called on to exist and thrive within such chaos and constant change. Agility seems to be the watchword for businesses and organizational champions in the twenty-first century.

Champions, however, flourish at such junctures and in such times because in a world of chaos and change, champions remain steady and grounded through a strong sense of self. Their foundational values and personal experiences help fend off the blows of failure, fear, intimidation, political agendas, and a barrage of new priorities. Their mettle helps them maneuver through corporate land mines toward corporate promised lands.

Figure 3.1 illustrates the process by which a person can begin to develop a values-based leadership platform. Not ironically, I call it the *mettle filter*.

Realize Your Ideal Self

The process of self-discovery, which leads to self-actualization, starts with who you aspire to be. In other words, who are you

Figure 3.1 The Mettle Filter

at your best? In still other words, regardless of circumstances or excuses, who is your ideal self?

As you're considering this question, separate yourself from your organization or company, your friends, your family, and any other external force that might influence your perspective. This question should be asked and answered only by you. After all, your family demands you to be different from your work self, which is different from what your friends demand you to be, and so on. This question requires an honest answer. Don't fall into the safe, culturally accepted, politically correct answer here for the sake of perceived acceptance.

For example, my ideal self is a pioneer or a trailblazer and a champion of the individual. I want to go into uncharted territory. I want to be open to anything that doesn't cause harm or ill will to someone else. I'm not a status quo guy in my ideal self. Sometimes I will break old rules and move beyond perceived boundaries. At my best, I show love to all people, enable the underdog, and challenge the top performer.

Who are you at your best?

Nature and Nurture

Your beautiful blue eyes, your crazy curly hair, and your predisposition to disease or addiction can arguably be blamed on your mother, father, or great-grandmother. Those innate physical and psychological characteristics come from a very complex DNA structure. DNA is made up of four chemicals that when paired together form a DNA "rung." There are 3 billion DNA working together to provide the instructions for building and maintaining your body of 100 trillion cells. This is your nature, and it is the blueprint for your existence.

Your "nurture" characteristics are developed through your social structure or from environmental factors. They are learned over time and enable you to grow toward maturity.

Scientists continue to debate about which is the more dominant influence on our growth and development. Thus far, most scientists have concluded that nature and nurture are equally important. It's a vital debate because many of our incorrect social perceptions result from assumptions about natural limitations. For example, women are physically smaller, and often present more sensitive behaviors than men do. This scientific "fact" contributed to unequal treatment of the "weaker sex." Nature was the excuse for the discrimination, but nurture was more likely the cause. We can't use nature or nurture as the basis for blanket perceptions or for attaching broad labels to people or things without filtering these perceptions through our ethical filters.

For champions, nature and nurture are influencers, but neither defines them. Champions are defined beyond their nature and their nurture, hence, the mettle filter illustration showing nature and nurture being filtered through personal beliefs and values, abilities and satisfactions, and purpose.

A child growing up in a broken home is not destined to suffer a broken marriage. An abusive childhood doesn't excuse an adult who abuses his or her own children. A person who grew up in a racially discriminating culture isn't forced to continue racial bigotry. Our personal experiences and setbacks may present barriers toward maturity, but maturity is an essential pursuit regardless of one's circumstances.

In the same way, nurture can be a great enabler toward maturity. Healthy homes should help produce future healthy homes. Charitable communities should produce future charitable communities.

But what about nature? Isn't it harder to overcome my hard-wired innate composition?

I wish I could answer this one, but I'm not qualified. There are, however, countless stories of people who have overcome physical disabilities or limitations to accomplish the extraordinary. Moses, who many believed to have stuttered, led Israel out of Egypt. Daniel "Rudy" Ruettiger, the 5-foot 6-inch, 165 pound football player, dreamed of playing football for the Notre Dame Fighting Irish. Against all physical odds, Rudy made the varsity team and made such an impression on the football players and fans that he was carried off the field after a game against Georgia Tech. Since then, no other player has been carried off the football field at Notre Dame.

My own son, Jax, has a birth defect in his brain. He is unable to control the trunk section of his body. Doctors said he may never walk, but that if he did, it would likely be assisted. Jax shunned his walker at age two. Now at age three, he's working on his fastball. That was incomprehensible.

Natural abilities and disabilities are very real. And while disabilities are physically or psychologically limiting and natural abilities are enabling, neither of them defines the human spirit or limits the possibilities.

Beliefs and Values

The point is not to debate the terms, but to facilitate a progressive process toward self-actualization. With that said, I readily admit that the terms used in the mettle filter are debatable and defined quite differently among scientists, scholars, and lay people. I also admit such self-actualization can never come from a book. My hope is to plant the seed so that you can begin taking the steps in your own journey toward self-actualization.

For the sake of progress, let's define beliefs as statements of fact about our perceived knowledge of truth. One's perceived knowledge of truth can come from three areas:

- Our own experiences
- Our adoption of scientific conclusions
- Our faith

Based on those three areas, it would be easy for us to form lots of beliefs. For example, I believe in gravity. If I drop a pen from my hand, it will fall to the ground assuming nothing gets in its way. Easy enough. However, I encourage you to move beyond simple truths and move to the core of your belief system. What are those core beliefs that give ultimate purpose to your existence or to your behavior? For example, you may believe:

In God as the creator of the universe.
That what goes around comes around.
That humanity is ultimately good.
That trust is the foundation of all healthy relationships.

List no more than five of your core beliefs below:

1. I believe _____
2. I believe _____
3. I believe _____
4. I believe _____
5. I believe _____

Your values are your beliefs in action. Your values are the behaviors that support your beliefs. You might say they are your nonnegotiables in life. Below is an example of how a belief and a value might be captured.

Belief. I believe that what goes around comes around.
Value. Therefore, I will treat others the way I want to be treated.

Remember that we are still in the "ideal self" phase of the self-actualization process. Just because you might not have lived out your values, doesn't mean that they aren't true values to you. We all fail many times. The great thing about having nonnegotiable values is that you're quick to recognize when you're off track and can, therefore, make the necessary adjustments.

Capture one to three values (behaviors in action) to support each belief.

Belief 1 _____
   1. Value _____
   2. Value _____
   3. Value _____
Belief 2 _____
   1. Value _____
   2. Value _____
   3. Value _____
Belief 3 _____
   1. Value _____
   2. Value _____
   3. Value _____
Belief 4 _____
   1. Value _____
   2. Value _____
   3. Value _____
Belief 5 _____
   1. Value _____
   2. Value _____
   3. Value _____

Come Alive and Uniquely Contribute

It's hard to find a business publication these days that doesn't contain an article dealing with talent or workforce development. Inevitably, vast attention is given to developing the proper skills of a worker or a leader that are necessary to close the performance gap in today's complex business setting. And rightly so. Collaboration, problem solving, creative thinking, analyzing, communication, market analysis, and managing change are absolutely critical skills needed in workforces that will help separate the winning organizations from the also-rans. More and more, companies are sweating the skill development game. Skills aren't being developed fast enough to enable workforces to match the demands of a constantly changing business environment. To speed development, companies often assign their best people to stretch assignments that push their top talent harder and faster toward their potential. Our research shows that champions are known to seek out and take on these extra assignments, especially extra or stretch assignments relating to developing others through mentoring, coaching, and knowledge transfer. My friend Robin is one such example and champion who accepted a stretch assignment to develop a deployment plan for an enterprisewide personal development system for thousands of team members. This was outside her normal role and was a stretch assignment that demanded more of her time. Her work was highly visible and successful. A promotion followed for her. Her achievement proved how champions can maintain and improve business results while prioritizing talent development.

Growth of abilities is obviously critical for an organization's success. As I note in Chapter 1, however, it doesn't take long for a competency model, initially created for its simplicity, to become extraordinarily dense as it works to cross the bounds of every need in every business unit. Competency models often end up containing so much that they provide little value. I have yet to see an organization adequately and efficiently implement a competency model that has met its desired objectives.

But the problem goes beyond skill development today. It's also a systems issue. Most development systems are closed systems, incapable of working with other systems. They cost too much, and they take up too many administration and information technology (IT) resources. Development systems aren't integrated, so calculating payout is impossible. And skill development systems, while supporting some of the most complex competency models, rarely line up with business strategy and performance metrics.

Tom Marshall, in his book *Understanding Leadership*, coined the term McLeaders to describe the end product of a development process. The premise of the term is that organizations are really good at developing people who eventually make up leadership teams where everyone looks the same, acts the same, and has the same capabilities. One's unique value is easily suppressed within the corporate environment behind a competency model supported by many disconnected systems. So the most critical workforce concerns today are being addressed by inadequate, linear systems and complex competency models with low life spans that fail to unleash the extraordinary and unique value of the individual. I could go on and on about this situation because my company has faced many of these challenges with our clients. But let's save it for another book.

Our goal here is to create organizational champions who are capable of transforming our businesses, our cultures, and our societies—not enabling yet another leadership competency model. In its simplest form, developing organizational champions is about a facilitated process toward self-actualization and then aligning the core composition of a champion with the needs of the organization.

Becoming self-actualized requires coming to grips with one's natural and compensatory abilities and weaknesses. Champions are good at assessing their abilities and acknowledging their weaknesses. SVI's research confirms that the highest performers rate themselves and their performance more closely to and aligned with ratings they receive from their peers, direct reports, and managers. The conclusion is that high performers have a better understanding of their own abilities than many others do.

Our research also concludes that champions are more accurate in their self-assessments because these high performers pursue feedback and embrace personal accountability. Champions shun image for accuracy. They make themselves vulnerable for the sake of improvement. They don't wait for annual performance reviews, but rather take ownership of their own development.

Can you list your abilities and weaknesses? How does your perception of your abilities align with other people's perception of your abilities? If you don't know, find out. Become vulnerable and ask. Don't feel the need to limit your gifts and abilities to your work or career demands. Expand to your gifts and abilities outside of work as well.

Abilities Category

What are you good at?

What do others say you're good at?

_____   _____

_____   _____

_____   _____

_____   _____

_____   _____

Both opinions—yours and theirs—count.

Another part of self-actualization is recognizing those things that bring you great satisfaction, lift your spirits, and cause those butterflies to erupt internally. In the words of Dr. Howard Thurman—a noted U.S. author, philosopher, and educator— "Don't ask yourself what the world needs, ask yourself what makes you come alive and go do that, because what the world needs is people who have come alive." How true. Can you imagine what our businesses and communities would be like if more people moved beyond their responsibilities and ignited their passions for the sake of the mission or the cause? Too many people have little to no idea what makes them come alive. They have no idea what builds the flame that ignites their heart. They don't know their heart's desire, and therefore, they fill their heart with anything that wanders by—a project, a problem, an affair, or perceived greener pastures that will take them anywhere but where they are today.

I have great empathy for those people who have no idea what brings them satisfaction. Many people I've interviewed tell me they are going through monotonous motions because they were told to do so. And when they were told to do so, they had nothing to counteroffer that would bring value to them and to their organization. They found no personal satisfaction in the task list. That task list brought value only through a paycheck.

Monotonously moving people, task-list-only people, are often unable to take on strategic assignments that fall outside the realm of their comfort zone, even though it would enhance critical business processes. One particular group that we work with had low satisfaction in their roles, and this group found it extremely difficult to engage in a project that asked them to step outside the normal job description. In fact, the majority of the members of the team was ready to give up right out of the gate. The inability of workers or leaders to find satisfaction in their role leads to a transactional and commoditized relationship between the employee and employer with the employee being available to the highest bidder. Companies that don't adopt a new view for engaging their workforce will find it harder and harder to keep good talent.

To create a loyal and healthy culture, value must be defined beyond the paycheck. It is both the responsibility of the employer and the employee to engage in conversations that bring personal alignment and satisfaction.

Think about what makes you come alive—relationships, adventure, research, travel, predictability, math, freedom, outdoors, debate, curiosity, manual labor, teamwork, design, chaos, whatever. If this question is difficult to answer, stop reading right now. Put down the book, find a tree on a hillside or some other isolated and relaxing spot, take nothing with you, get really bored, let your mind empty, and then recall the exciting memories from your past. When you've captured them, connect with them. Do you see any themes? Do the memories involve other people, or are you alone? Were they times of excitement or of quiet reflection? Did you find fulfillment in a courageous challenge, or were you personally invested in a worthy cause? Write some of the themes in the space below. By the way, you can't ask others for help here. For this one, you're on your own.

Satisfactions Category

What makes you come alive—your satisfactions?

_____

_____

_____

_____

_____

_____

_____

Organizational champions, like those we discuss in Chapter 2, work much of what they love into what they do. Kim Partoll of AOL loves relationships and leads through them. Jeff Webster of Tyson loves innovation and leads through creative thought and application. Lou Gerstner of IBM loves to overcome challenges and leads through bold moves, courage, and a strong sense of mission. Do you need to bring more of what you love into more of what you do? If so, what are some steps you can take toward accomplishing that goal?

Realize a Sense of Purpose

As we've discussed, a champion isn't shaped by circumstance, the flavor of the day, or the political agenda. Champions have a strong rudder that can cut through the intense waves caused by even the most severe corporate storms. A business casualty is a blip on a champion's radar as he or she remains poised and steady. Why? Because champions are deeply rooted beyond the business, and they believe in things beyond themselves. They don't see themselves or their organizations as the end of the story, but rather as part of a much grander scheme and purpose. They strive to align their behaviors with their beliefs. Because they are deeply rooted, they are authentic, consistent, and trusted.

Champions combine their beliefs, values, abilities, and satisfactions to form a strong sense of purpose. They know why they get out of bed every morning, and they live minute by minute, day by day, toward that purpose. And nothing gets in the way. They know who they are at the core and what they were meant for in life. They know why they exist—what purpose they serve. Your purpose can be described as your personal brand. I know what I get when I fly Southwest Airlines—a fun and freeing flying experience. I know when I positively have to get something delivered overnight, I order up FedEx. When people order you up, what do they get? When someone pulls you off the shelf, what do you consistently provide—a pioneer or trailblazer, an analyzer or communicator, a listener or a minister? What is unique about who you are? What differentiates you from others, and how do you deliver your uniqueness to the world?

Review your beliefs, your values, your abilities, and your satisfactions categories, and identify common themes that resonate in each of these areas. Does a theme appear in more than one or two of these categories? Do you see a relationship theme in both your values and your satisfactions categories, or a teaching theme in both your beliefs and your abilities categories? Do you value methodical thinking and are you good analytically? Are you a creative thinker with a desire to pursue new opportunities? Identify the themes that appear more dominant in these categories and write them down here.

_____

_____

_____

_____

_____

_____

Once you've captured these themes, see if you can form a personal brand statement from them. Just like product brands, your personal brand statement should be no more than a sentence or two—not a paragraph. Make it simple enough that you can recall it even during the most intense times in your day.

As you develop your brand statement, remember this: The world's strongest brands have been carefully crafted, methodically developed, invested in, tested, and protected over time. Brands are important for the success of the product. Brand attributes manage intended perception, and brand managers are intentional and diligent in the development of a brand. Isn't your personal brand even more important? Don't let the world label you. Solidify your involvement and leadership in a way that personally aligns with who you are and how you contribute.

Write your personal brand statement—your purpose.

_____

_____

_____

_____

I understand that this might be a difficult process, but take the time to do it. To help you with an example, I've included my themes that fit these categories and my resulting personal brand, or purpose statement. Realize that these are my beliefs, values, abilities, satisfactions, and personal brand statement. They are not yours, and they shouldn't be. I'm not presenting my themes as ones you should embrace but simply offer them as a model to guide you.

My Core Beliefs

1. God loves me.
2. Life is a precious gift.
3. My faith is my hope.

Therefore I will (values):

1. Trust God's influence
2. Serve others always
3. Live passionately and adventurously

My abilities are:

1. Leadership
2. Coaching
3. Counseling
4. Creativity
5. Building

My satisfactions are:

1. Relationships
2. Adventure
3. Competing
4. Traveling

Based on the themes within these categories, I formed the following personal brand or purpose statement:

> Love God, love people, love life, and boldly journey ahead.

Everything I do should support that statement. Because of that statement, I will go before others and try new things. I'll consider the benefit of others in my decisions, and I'll invest in my spiritual growth. My brand statement resonates with my ideal self. I'm a pioneer or trailblazer because I'm a lover of life. I champion the individual because I love people. That statement serves what I do in my career, how I treat my wife and kids, and how I spend my leisure time.

Summary

Becoming enlightened is the first step toward becoming an organizational champion because the process starts with you. Naturally living out your core propensity is necessary for personal efficiency and effectiveness. Don't diminish the importance of personal growth and improvement, however. But realize that your best improvement will grow from your core sense of self. If you're an introvert, you'll likely never be a natural extrovert—but you might learn to communicate better. If you're an academic, you might not be an artist (though these aren't mutually exclusive)—but you might learn to think more creatively.

Those who fail to understand who they are often fail to lead naturally, always trying to fit into someone else's leadership mold. This only leads to frustration and inefficiency. Through perspective and understanding, embrace who you are naturally—pursue growth from your core, and unleash your unique and valuable gifts.

Discovering yourself gives you a newfound significance and sense of purpose. Discovering yourself gives you more freedom to move through life and run wild as you've defined your own playing field. Discovering yourself gives you new energy and passion that allow you to bring your best to any situation.

CHAPTER 4

BE AN ENERGIZER
OF THE CULTURE

M ark Cuban is the cofounder of HDNet and has made more than a billion dollars in the field of technology, but he is better known as the controversial owner of the NBA's Dallas Mavericks. When he took over ownership of the Mavericks in 2000, he brought a new level of enthusiasm and a new energy to the team, and ticket sales exploded. When the season started, some were surprised to find Cuban shunning the skybox for the courtside seats. He would often scream at the refs and exchange high fives with a player after a monster jam. Technical fouls have been called on him a number of times when he vocally—and vociferously—objected to a referee's call. Cuban, obviously, was not your typical NBA team owner.

Because of his unusual behavior, Cuban began to draw criticism from some commentators, NBA league officials, fans, the media, and even his players. There is no question that he has made some interesting choices and questionable decisions. But no one can doubt his passion. His powerful emotions unleash his drive to win. And no one can question his success. Prior to his purchase of the team in January 2000, the Mavericks' all-time winning percentage was a mere 40 percent. Under Cuban, the Mavs are continuously in the playoffs, have appeared in the NBA championship game, and boast a regular season winning percentage of 70 percent. His emotional energy helped usher in quite a turnaround for the team.

Cuban's passion gives him great courage and determination in pursuit of his goals for the team. And in that regard he's not unique. Many of today's most admired CEOs and champions display these emotional attributes and habitual bursts of energy. These leaders or champions didn't discover their emotions, passions, visions, dreams, or drive after accepting their leadership post. CEOing doesn't open the door to self-awareness, understanding, courage, vulnerability, and a newfound freedom for emotional engagement. Those qualities led to their achieving such high positions. There are thousands of examples of people who have taken a passionate approach in relentless pursuit of their ideas and ideals well before they became "something." And those attributes were, and still are, vital to their current and continued success.

Great leaders seem to know instinctively how to use their emotional energy to drive others toward desired results. They know when to be soft and sensitive and when to show their teeth. Martin Luther King, Jr.'s profound sensitivity to injustice and its impact on individual lives translated into a passion so formidable that it brought a nation to its knees. Princess Diana's smile lit up the world, and the world embraced her for her genuineness and sincerity, but she could be politically indomitable when it came to defending suffering children in Angola and

Bosnia. Ronald Reagan charmed a nation—political friends and foes alike—with his confident smile and down-home one-liners; meanwhile his staff knew him as the toughest boss they'd ever worked for. In the popular imagination, Mother Teresa was a quiet spirit with an outsized heart and little physical strength. Her manner of speaking, her tenderness, the clothes she wore, her diminutive appearance—these were her trademarks. But when Albanian-born Agnes Gonxha Bojaxhiu marched into a roomful of executive bankers and called them on the carpet for unethical practices, she showed another side of Mother Teresa. She was a lion when she needed to be. And she roamed the most dangerous environments on earth, putting her own safety at risk to pursue her goals: defending and ministering to others.

These were sensitive people—sensitive to the world, the times, the human heart. Sensitivity was at the very core of the gifts we celebrate in them. But don't stop there. Add their ability to know when to give full rein to their emotions, and those attributes combined is what made them household names, and even shapers of history. That's what made them champions.

Through these examples, I don't mean to imply that showing emotion is always a showing of teeth. Sometimes champions may need to kick the water cooler to inspire action. But much of the time they show their emotions through enthusiasm and excitement. By fully embracing a change or new initiative and showing their excitement for it, they inspire their teams and their companies.

Champions are quick to show their enthusiasm as they set the tone right out of the gate. In fact, our research shows that champions are significantly more energizing over the long term than nonchampions. Their vulnerability and self-worth allow them to be the first to offer their excitement for a yet-to-be-determined outcome. They bring the energy even before the energy is deserved in order to set the tone, build the commitment, and create the drive.

Rob Rivenburgh of Mars, a leading marketing and communications company, took a big risk on SVI when he championed our firm in the midst of an economic punch to the gut for companies in the advertising and marketing industry. For Rob, there was no better time to commit to developing Mars's people. Mars had just set some enormous corporate goals, adjusted its business model, and rebranded its organization. Rob knew that the final component would be to build a strong culture around these big and significant changes.

Mars had never embarked on a cultural development program, and needless to say, many of those at the top were skeptical. But Rob championed the effort, pushed the process, and accepted complete responsibility for its outcomes. At every turn, Rob communicated his excitement and built energy within Mars. He presented the vision and his expected outcomes. He micromanaged every detail to ensure progress—and every progression ignited more enthusiasm, which eventually extended beyond Rob. Soon even those at the highest levels had caught the fever.

Rob's leadership paved the way for members of his entire team to express their passion and emotion at work, which ignited a dynamic and productive culture. Adult-to-adult accountability conversations began taking place, tense debates weren't culturally consequential, but rather healthy and respectable, and personal engagement and team commitment immediately improved.

Leading with emotion, therefore, doesn't only mean roaring like a lion. Nor does it always require a rah-rah approach. What it must be is a sincere expression of strong feelings in a way that inspires others. Some champion leaders rarely raise their voices. But, when necessary, they say exactly what they feel, and their honesty and emotional openness ignites others to take action.

Every reader of this book has energy and emotion. It's physiological.

Everyone dreams of progress. It's worthy and human.

Everyone has ideas ready to be unleashed. It's human nature.

And yet we often hesitate to show our emotion, energy, and even humanity in the workplace.

Organizational Champions Engage Their Emotions

According to Daniel Goleman, Richard Boyatzis, and Annie McKee, leaders in emotional intelligence studies and authors of the book *Primal Leadership*, our emotional energy naturally and scientifically resonates with others. *Primal Leadership* maintains that effective leaders use their emotions to ignite and synchronize a group toward a mission, helping members of the group increase their personal engagement and find a new level of meaning in their work.

Primal Leadership goes on to suggest that our mood and our tone as a leader are critical components in our behavior as we strive to move others. It's not just what a leader does that's important, but how a leader does it. Why? It's how we are designed. Scientists who study brain structure have identified a functional behavior that occurs within the limbic system, our emotional centers in the brain. This functional behavior is an open-loop system, which is different from a closed-loop system, such as the circulatory system that transfers nutrients throughout our body. In a closed system, what others do around us has no impact on our own systems. How your body digests protein has nothing to do with how my body does it. However, open systems depend largely on external sources to manage themselves. How you feel will influence how I feel. Therefore, we rely on other people for our emotional stability.

How leaders use their emotions has a significant impact on the behaviors of others by transferring greater emotional energy to the group. But, you might ask, is this a good thing? It seems that all we have are more emotional people. Is that an advantage to business performance and results beyond simply ushering positive or negative vibes within the culture?

Emotional Energy Delivers Stronger Results

Earlier I made the claim that organizational champions achieve stronger business results than do nonchampions. This observation was confirmed as my team compared the business results—such as sales, operational performance, profits, customer satisfaction, and turnover—of old-style leaders (transactional, linear-minded, competency-driven only) with those of organizational champions. Champions who were emotionally

energizing and inspirational achieved the best business results.

Our research finds that organizational champions energize their teams, and their teams respond by embracing new challenges and persevering through barriers toward their goals. What I love about inspiration is that when I'm inspired, I increase my commitment and engagement, I seem to develop more resolve, I'm more motivated to act, and my energy level is amplified.

But it's not just a stronger engagement and drive that benefit from emotions and energy. Research suggests that our emotions are essential for our making good decisions and choices. According to a study by Myeong-Gu Seo of the University of Maryland's business school and Lisa Feldman Barrett of Boston College's psychology department, the most effective decision makers are those who had strong feelings and emotions while making decisions. These findings contradict the popular belief that feelings can drive linear and close-minded thinking. It is believed that emotional leaders will allow their emotions to get in the way of a healthy dialogue where hearing the other points is just as important as one's own contribution. The study addressed emotional biases and concluded that good decision makers, while emotionally charged, were able to prevent their emotions from impeding their ability to reason. Therefore, it's not the emotions that get in the way of a good decision. Bad decisions come from bad decision makers—emotional or not.

Antonio Damasio is an internationally acclaimed behavioral neurologist and neuroscientist who founded and leads USC's Brain and Creativity Institute. Through his work, he has taken the importance of engaging emotions to make good decisions to another level. From his research and observations of patients who had brain damage of the prefrontal cortical (area of the brain responsible for cognitive behaviors, personality expression, and moderating correct social behavior), he claims that in the absence of emotion, it isn't just difficult but rather impossible to make any decisions at all. These patients weren't able to decide because they weren't able to experience emotions. While I understand that comparing severely brain-damaged patients with corporate leaders isn't necessarily a fair one, the point is still relevant. The point being that science connects our emotional capacity to our ability to make decisions, but it doesn't determine the outcome of these decisions.

Now let's talk energy. It's simple science. Human beings gain energy from sources such as the sun and the food we eat. Our energy can be exerted and released based on physiological impacts from environmental circumstances such as wind or gravity. But our emotions are also a source of energy. Our energy output can change based on our mood, how rested or how motivated we are.

When I awoke this morning, it was raining heavily. While I was lying in bed listening to the rain, I didn't feel motivated to get up and start working. But the fact that I have a deadline for this book overruled those environmental factors. I consciously moved my body out of bed, got dressed, and visited the Silver Joe's Coffee drive-thru. Ah, caffeine.

Fuel for our bodies creates the necessary energy we require to take action according to our needs or desires.

Epinephrine, also known as adrenaline, is a hormone and neurotransmitter that is necessary for our bodies to respond energetically to stressful situations. The brain tells the body to release epinephrine into our bloodstream from the adrenal glands when we experience stress from danger, love, opportunities, or deadlines. The release of epinephrine boosts the supply of oxygen to the brain and muscles, giving them the energy they need to react.

Therefore, you might say that epinephrine is our emotional source of energy.

We lose energy when we lose emotions. We lose the drive when we lose the drama. This is fundamental and foundational. Yet, today we are seeing the complete suppression of passion. Our organizations and leaders often lecture us that our emotions get in the way of smart decisions and that they cloud our judgment. We're asked to be detached and, therefore, we have become passionless and emotionless for the sake of safety or tradition, or for the sake of not embarrassing ourselves or our organizations. How many times have you heard something similar to the following conversation?

Sarah: Joe got really emotional in the meeting today, didn't he?

David: Yeah. He needs to check his emotions at the door. His emotions got in the way of a very strategic discussion.

Sarah: He's so dramatic. Doesn't he understand the way things get done around here?

David: My advice to him is to lay low. It's not worth the risk. This company's been doing this standard of practice for 50 years.

Sarah: Oh well, back to the grind. Thank God it's Friday. Five o'clock can't get here fast enough.

I'm not pushing for unbridled, out-of-control emotional outbursts. My question is have we gone too far in suppressing them? And my answer is yes. Our research finds that leaders who significantly lack energy and passion underperform in their roles compared to energized and passionate leaders. Furthermore, studies show that EQ (emotional intelligence quotient) is a more relevant indicator than IQ (intelligence quotient) in determining one's success. Compare Herb Kelleher, Southwest Airlines' emotional leader, to past Continental Airlines CEO Frank Lorenzo. Herb led through vulnerability and humility. Lorenzo was guarded by a tight inner circle and led Continental Airlines into bankruptcy in 1983.

Research suggests that the most successful CEOs lead under the premise of people first, strategy second. And people relate emotionally. It's important to note that this form of leadership is not limited to just the CEO position, but such value placed on emotion is found at all levels within an organization. Time and time again I find those people with relational or emotional energy to be more responsive and more productive than those without such energy. Work moves with them; big things get done. They're excited, and they excite others involved. Our research shows that those leaders who are constantly suppressing their emotions are rarely able to move critical projects forward successfully until they're forced to do so by their superior. We also have found that these people seek support from their superiors not only to move them, but to move their team as well. The nonchampion's lack of passion or enthusiasm affects many throughout the execution of the project.

Jerry Yang is one of the founders of Yahoo! and its CEO until January 2009. If you haven't noticed lately, Yahoo! is in a steep decline in value, and Yang wasn't able to right the ship. After staving off a buyout attempt by Microsoft, he found his company much worse for the wear. Microsoft offered to purchase Yahoo! for $33 per share ($10 more per share than the company was valued at the time). Yahoo's stock at the time of this writing is valued at a mere $11 per share. In May 2008, Yang delivered a "state of the union" speech to Yahoo! employees. Many, who relied on Yahoo! for their livelihood, were hoping for the answers that were going to elevate the company once again. But when Yang took the stage, people described him as appearing resigned and beleaguered. During his talk, Yang rambled aimlessly about direction, and the audience was quickly losing confidence. Yang's talk needed to be a rallying cry for "we're focused," but instead, the talk communicated "we're finished." Yang had no charisma, and the lack of charisma translated to a lack of confidence that was later confirmed when he told an interviewer after the speech, "I'll never be a CEO again."

Enthusiasm doesn't necessarily call for a loud rah-rah project cheerleader, but one can definitely capture the importance of the effort by one's emotional commitment. SVI's research finds that a significant relationship and correlation exist between those who are most inspirational with those who are most productive. This finding isn't a slight comparison; this is a solid discovery. Champions don't raise ideas with passion and then fear they'll be seen as being overly emotional and therefore not rational. They refuse to keep silent for the sake of being seen as a "team player," someone who goes along without attracting too much attention, who abides by the system. They aren't afraid to raise too big a fuss that just might raise the eyebrows—or even the ire—of an upper-level manager.

I was struck by a story of legendary pro football coach Bill Walsh, who, in his early years, was an assistant coach for Paul Brown with the Cincinnati Bengals. According to Andrew O'Toole's biography titled *Paul Brown*, Walsh was considered even then to be the most gifted member of the staff. It was assumed that when Brown stepped down as head coach and limited himself to the owner's office, Walsh would take over the team. Brown admired Walsh but felt that he could be "too emotional," which members of the media inferred meant "too hard to control." When Brown did step down, he chose Bill Johnson as his successor. Walsh quit the team, and in a few years was head coach of the San Francisco 49ers, where he led his team to three Super Bowl victories—two of them, ironically, over Brown's Bengals.

Stories like this one are not uncommon in business. Leading with emotion can create a clash of egos. But champions find a way to make it work. They seize opportunities and put their emotions into the effort. An enlightened manager will recognize the benefit and celebrate it. If Paul Brown had done that, he might have gotten the world championships with Walsh. Instead, he got none.

Keeping with the sports theme, tennis is an etiquette sport, especially at its premier event, Wimbledon. But I always appreciate how much the fans enjoy and even cheer at the periodic vocal bursts of agony or elation by the competitors. Why do we, as fans, enjoy the outbursts of emotions?

We enjoy them because we literally catch their emotions for ourselves and then connect with them, thus becoming emotionally in sync with the athlete. We see the agony or determination of the underdog and then suddenly switch our allegiance from the favorite. We see frustration in a player and feel it ourselves. We respond to the grunt as a player tries to put more energy into a shot. We connect with a player's enthusiastic fist pump after a well-played volley.

The same dynamic occurs every day in the meeting rooms where champions lead their teams. The champion's passion fuels new initiatives that the team embraces. Sparked by that passion, team members become more creative and effective, adding their own ideas and executing the details far better than they would if they were simply handed a task list.

An interesting note: our research found that while organizational champions give significantly more emotional energy and inspiration to their teams to enable them, these champions aren't dependent on others for energy and enablement. While others depend on relationships to drive their commitment, reactions, and attitudes, champions don't need such support. They have the ability to elevate themselves beyond the negative moods and transcend the energy drains from others and are able to maintain focus and drive. Just as champions don't wait for the opportunities, they create them; champions don't wait for someone to spark their passion. They rarely depend on anyone for their actions. They are often inspired by others, but their inspiration can extend beyond others to a different or higher plain as well.

Organizational Champions Are Inspired and Inspiring

To be inspiring, you must first be inspired. *Inspired* literally means "breathed upon." And I'm most inspired when I experience those moments in life that literally take my breath away. Many of those moments, for me, occur in the deserts of Arizona at sunset. One of my best friends lives in Scottsdale, Arizona, and I visit him a few times a year. Todd has become an even closer friend since he bought two Suzuki dirt bikes. During a visit, he and I wake up early in the morning, load the dirt bikes onto the trailer, throw the gear in the back of the truck, fill our backpacks with granola bars and Gatorade, and head to one of a thousand trails that run through the desert. Our rides are often interrupted by periodic stops on various mountain peaks, as the Arizona landscapes are too brilliant to zoom past without taking notice. Inevitably, by the end of the day we can't help but reflect upon the amazing beauty of this place and upon the rich blessings of our lives. Recently, during one of our moments of reflection, we talked about inspiration. What is it, why do we love it when we get it, why don't more people give it?

Inspiration is a nebulous term. Psychologists seem to have avoided the study of it, for the most part. Most research I find on it deals with the inner personal workings of a creative process. Sigmund Freud, when studying artists and their inspiration, found them to be fundamentally special or fundamentally wounded. Okay. That fits. Aren't we inspired by those we view as special or by those who have survived great emotional or physical tragedy? We either aspire to be like them for their talents, or we would hate to be them for the wounds they've suffered.

In modern psychology, inspiration is generally seen as an entirely internal process beyond one's control. From my perspective, a workable definition might be that inspiration is an unconscious burst of feeling beyond one's control. If it's unconscious, then we never know precisely when it will come. But we will know it when it decides to show up because it will likely be expressed through our emotions and even felt physiologically through a tingle on our skin or a blush on our cheeks. If it's beyond our control, then we can't demand its presence.

The drivers of inspiration seem to be life experiences and enlightenment. But I can't argue against the fact that some people might innately be more easily inspired than others and, therefore, more inspiring.

I do believe, however, that all of us can increase the opportunities we have to be inspired. Our research shows that champions are more curious and seek more opportunities for inspiration than nonchampions. By finding more of these opportunities to live in breathtaking moments, our chances for inspiration increase. It starts by intentionally detaching yourself from the routine and pursuing those things that make you come alive. Remember the quote from Howard Thurman in Chapter 3: "Don't ask yourself what the world needs, ask yourself what makes you come alive and go do that, because what the world needs is people who have come alive."

If you want to be a champion and inspire others, ask yourself what makes you come alive. Recall moments when you felt inspired. Accomplishments seem to ignite inspiration. So do moments of discovery and shared feelings.

Seek more such moments. Seek new experiences, especially ones that might make you uncomfortable and force you to adapt and grow.

Organizational Champions Use Their Experiences to Fuel Passion

Seth was a successful attorney in one of the leading law firms in the South. Needless to say, he was busy, and his work was important. Seth had a friend who traded a comfortable life and career in the United States for a benevolent cause in Southeast Africa, helping teach impoverished and disease-stricken communities how to farm and, thus, restoring health to these communities. For years, Seth promised to visit his friend and experience the cause. For years, he put it off because of his busy work schedule. But not last year. He finally made time to spend eight days in Southeast Africa with his friend.

And he was changed forever.

Upon his return, Seth and I had dinner with our wives to hear about the adventures in Africa. During dinner, it was easy to see that Seth was not the same. This professional attorney whose job it is to play it cool couldn't get through the appetizer without breaking down as he told story after story of his experience with the Africans. He gained new perspectives and insights. His views on life were richer and more profound.

Seth is still a successful attorney. But now even his normal business stories are vibrant with color. He is much more vulnerable and self-reflective in his relationships, and he shows a new enthusiasm and gusto for life. His experience ignited his inspiration. As a result, people are more drawn to him. I know I am. Inspiration doesn't require life change, but it seems to require life embracement. People who are inspirational tend to have more people wanting to connect with them in order to experience more of what these inspirational people have to offer.

Organizational champions reflect on, embrace, and use their experiences, good and bad, to fuel their passion. Their experiences make them more inspirational. Seth's experience in Africa was intense. He battled illness, hunger, exhaustion, and anguish. He experienced times of extreme sorrow, compassion, and abundant joy. And because of it, Seth became more inspirational.

Having intense emotional experiences may not be required to become a champion, but according to some theorists, it helps. Warren Bennis and Robert Thomas, in their book *Geeks and Geezers*, conclude that crucible experiences help shape the most extraordinary people. Bennis, one of the patriarchs of leadership, and Thomas, a senior fellow with Accenture's Institute for Strategic Change, interviewed more than 40 leaders whom they deem either "geeks" (aged 21 to 34) or "geezers" (aged 70 to 82) to evaluate the effect of era on values and success. Bennis and Thomas discovered that the two groups varied in terms of their ambitions, heroes, and family lives, but members of both sets shared one common experience: all have "undergone at least one intense, transformational experience," which the authors call a "crucible."

These crucibles become critical learning moments in a person's life. For champions, their mettle has been tested, and they have crawled out of the muck, better enabled to ignite and unleash their extraordinary influence and impact, and they inspire us through their ability to overcome and grow through newfound wisdom.

Organizational Champions Make Things Personal

Because of SVI's research division, we're fortunate to talk to a lot of people at various levels of management and who are various ages. Though we speak to people at companies large and small and in locations throughout the world, the results are surprisingly similar on certain subjects.

One subject that frequently arises is the cultural dilemma companies face today of having five generations working together. It seems that almost everyone has an opinion and perception of the other generation. And in my experience, there is little grace and appreciation for "the other" generation of workers. Older generations struggle to relate to the work ethic and perceived lack of responsibility of the younger generations. And the younger generations struggle to care what older generations think about them. Acknowledging the risk of categorizing people, in its simplest form and generally speaking, older generations tend to prioritize progress, and younger generations tend to prioritize purpose. And if one prioritizes a sense of purpose, then usually it's personal.

But somehow, the younger generations have created or allowed an image of themselves as disloyal, selfish, and entitled. I've had countless discussions with frustrated older-generation managers who say about a younger-generation employee, "He's been here three months, and he's demanding his next promotion already. Hell, he doesn't even show up to work on time."

I finally got some insight into the situation in an unlikely place: the Amtrak from New York to Boston. As an aside, let me say it's the best way to travel. First-class seats, spacious work desks, a full café and bar area, and beautiful views of neighboring cities and the coastline the whole way. I was fortunate enough to sit across the aisle from people in their mid-twenties who were talking about life, marriage, and career opportunities. I'm a generation Xer, fitting in between baby boomers and Ys. But I work with vets, baby boomers, Xs, Ys, nets, and millennials.

So I investigate. And the New York to Boston train was a perfect opportunity for me to ask yet another group of twenty-somethings about their perception of their image, and to capture their responses.

My first question is always about their thoughts on the perception of their generation. Not surprisingly, their responses to this question are consistent with other responses I get from other discussions I've had with other members of younger generations.

"I'm not really like my generation," they say.

In that one statement, there is no defense of the generalization cast upon them, but rather an acknowledgment and agreement of the perception. The problem is that of more than 100 people I've formally and informally interviewed from the younger generations, none of them claims to possess the perceived attributes and characteristics commonly identified with their generation. So the perceptions are accurate, but the reality is different from the perceptions. The perception is that they are disloyal. The reality is that they are extremely loyal to the things they care about. So are champions. But even more, we find that champions, over traditional leaders, strive to make this personal connection to the company mission for every member of their team.

It seems younger generations do value hard work, and they aren't necessarily disloyal. They might feel entitled, but that's because they've grown up in comfortable circumstances, many of them living in big houses, and they've rarely experienced anything other than abundance.

It occurred to me on the train that they're the humanitarian generation, altruistically dialed in. Rich rewards are not the key driver to loyalty with younger generations. They don't jump from one company to another for money or promotions—though that might be the claim. According to *Fortune* magazine's May 2007 article by Nadira A. Hira on twenty-somethings titled "Manage Us, Puh-leeze," twenty-somethings work for a purpose, or they don't work at all. They saw what "work" was to their parents, how their parents' career pursuits often left them empty emotionally, stressed physically, and unsecured professionally.

Money, therefore, isn't at the top of their priority list. They want purpose and contribution. This generation of professionals seems to emphasize those things in life that give them personal meaning. Today, work must be worthy of personal investment. Future workers are going to have a very difficult time separating their personal life from their professional life. These worlds are merging.

Even with the tough economy and social volatility that exists, record numbers of philanthropists, humanitarians, and missionaries are signing up for medical work in the Amazon, hunger relief efforts in Mexico, and natural disaster relief wherever and whenever a disaster hits.

When a twenty-something is aligned personally behind an organizational mission and his or her contribution is recognized, I'm willing to bet that loyalty isn't an issue.

And "making it personal" works well for all generations. In fact, it's a core principle for organizational champions. The work is not simply a job that leads to money. It's a personal mission with a purpose that aligns with their values and passions. Though the younger generation more obviously embodies this approach, it works for everyone.

I've worked with a man named Jim who personifies this principle of champions. Jim isn't twenty-something. He's quite a bit older. But he's a compassionate entrepreneur who sets up new businesses in many needy and underprivileged communities. His businesses bring hope to these communities as hundreds of new jobs are brought in through manufacturing opportunities. His business is personal to him, and he finds significant meaning and purpose in his work as he travels to these communities often—not for oversight necessarily, but for ministry. Jim's compassion is contagious to his employees inside and outside these communities as well. He doesn't pay the most. In fact, he doesn't pay that well at all. But his people are committed because they've connected to the same sense of purpose and mission Jim has. Jim's experience suggests that those people whose purpose in life is consistent with their purpose for work will be the most extraordinary leaders, personally committed and loyal to the mission.

Organizational Champions Energize Others

When things are personal, it's not too much of a stretch to allow your emotions to radiate through your communications. For years, we've seen effective leaders lead successfully without being great or even good communicators. Communicating to energize is not about charisma. It's not about eloquence.

It's about giving yourself to others through your words, experiences, and expressions.

I'm not an eloquent, inspiring speaker by any means. In fact, the pressure and responsibility of communicating is uncomfortable for me. I often question any relevance of importance for what I have to say. After all, people are smart and are being preached to or marketed to at every turn. What could I possibly add to the noise? But a drama teacher gave me a piece of advice I'll never forget. She said to look at your communications as a gift, not a presentation. She went on to explain that, by communicating my ideas or insights through emotions, I'm being vulnerable and opening myself up for entire audiences to evaluate, critique, embrace, or completely dismiss. Only through the giving of a gift can I make my communications about my audience and not about me. Authentically communicating with passion, energy, and vulnerability is not a selfish pursuit for popularity or recognition, but rather a complete pouring out of yourself for the sake of others. Nothing is more inspiring. Nothing will ignite a culture more than seeing a leader speak from the heart with conviction, passion, and vulnerability. One's conviction and emotional energy inspire others to risk, bring ideas, pursue a much higher platform of success—accomplishing more than anyone ever expected—shoot for the moon, and settle for nothing less.

Organizational champions aren't afraid to bring the drama, but they use it in order to move organizations, not to tear people down. Their sensationalism gives them great power in leadership.

I've had countless conversations with employees whose engagement is directly tied to their boss's influence or lack thereof. We often find that people don't leave companies; they leave people in those companies. These dissatisfied workers aren't necessarily dissatisfied with the company, but they find their boss's demotivating far from energizing, and definitely not inspirational. Not surprisingly, neither are they. Over the years, these employees have struggled with engagement, self worth, and a lack of passion in almost all areas of their life—the impact of a suppressing boss often extends beyond eight to five. In support of this, SVI's research shows that people who lack energy and motivation for their team are rated lower by their direct reports in many performance and leadership categories compared to people who have these motivating qualities. Those unmotivated employees are products of a typically uninspiring corporate culture. While these unmotivated employees are partly to blame, I can't help but also blame the approach to selection, development, and reward for leadership in our organizations today.

Intellectual and technical skills are overemphasized in the succession plans. Those intellectual and technical skills served the leader well in lower-level leadership roles with greater emphasis on projects and processes. But as the leader moved into the executive ranks, intellectual and technical skills can go only so far, especially in today's highly complex business environment.

In fact, in our research on desired champion attributes, respondents rated technical skills and expertise at the bottom of a list of 19 attributes.

It's time for companies to rid themselves of organizational constraints that add to the suppression of emotions among leaders and embrace the energy brought by organizational champions.

Summary

How effectively are you engaging your emotional energy? Are you using your emotions to drive results, or are you suppressing them for personal concern or protection? Realize that champions are out in front with their energy and emotions, offering them as gifts to move others.

I encourage you to do the same. Risk vulnerability for the sake of progress. Rather than detach yourself from an initiative or relationship for self-preservation, personally engage and bring your energy in order to influence others toward acceptance or involvement. If you believe in a direction, fight the urge to wade slowly into the water with the others. Be the first to make a splash. Mark Cuban did. So did Martin Luther King, Jr.,

Princess Diana, and countless others. I'm betting that many of your personal heroes did to. They didn't wait to be called or affirmed. They energized others through their emotions, and their emotions ignited their actions. They were the example and the inspiration for others who were hesitant to move.

CHAPTER *5*

CONNECT THROUGH MUTUALLY BENEFICIAL RELATIONSHIPS

C hampions don't go it alone. They connect. Their ability to connect with others helps them and their organizations become more successful. A champion's connection with others is built through mutually beneficial pursuits, cooperation, trust, and an intense and disproportionate attention on their producers.

Champions Pursue Mutually Beneficial Values

In the business world we hear a lot about win-win. It's used so often, in fact, when deals are discussed that it's become a cliché. Unfortunately, it's not always said with sincerity. We're taught that in business we should be concerned about winning. If the other person wins too, then great. If not, well, we hope we haven't burned a bridge, but we're not going to lose a lot of sleep over it.

Often this focus on our own winning is considered human nature. It's not, however, an organizational champion's nature. Organizational champions subscribe to a higher moral code. They operate under an ambitious agenda—mutual benefit and global good. They want to win as much as anyone, but it's equally important that the other person win too. Pepsi wants to sell more Pepsi, but it also wants to deliver clean water to suffering countries—Pepsi wins, and society wins. Wrangler wants to sell more jeans, but it also wants to grow the entire jeanswear category—Wrangler wins and so do the retailers and even Wrangler's competitors. Google wants to dominate the online advertising business, but it also wants to improve the lives of its employees and their families—Google wins and so do its employees and their families.

Love your neighbor as yourself is not just a moral principle; it's also a scientific advantage as we discuss in this chapter. This moral principle, now and forever, applies to businesses and their leaders. So do the advantages. Our research at SVI shows that leaders who were unsuccessful in their roles lacked genuine care for others and weren't intentional about working toward the greater good of the team. Rather, their drive was self-centered.

As I point out in Chapter 1, companies that do good have a greater return on shareholder wealth than traditional companies focused only on profit and loss. Mutual benefit doesn't mean an altruistic mindset with me losing and you winning. Mutual benefit means we both win and so might others, hence a global good. The Starbucks brand is big with me. I enjoy a grande coffee with hazelnut almost every morning. I'm a loyal buyer—Starbucks wins. I can enjoy a convenient coffee experience—my win. Starbucks, through its featured "GOOD

Sheets" from GOOD, their Ethos products, their Shared Planet campaign, and their in-store signage, educates me every time I walk through the door on the needs of our planet and the good works being accomplished by various organizations supported by Starbucks—society wins. When all the wins are brought together, it's a global win.

It may seem an unlikely choice, given the shots it takes from the media and watchdog groups, but let's begin with Wal-Mart as an example. It often exchanges the pole position with Exxon Mobil for the largest company in the world, and its success is undeniable, in large part because of its focus on "every day low prices." However, Wal-Mart has been going through a major transformation.

I've had the opportunity to work with and participate in some transformation discussions with Wal-Mart and have found that the change from "every day low prices" to "Save money. Live better" isn't just a matter of updating a marketing slogan. It's a departure from many of Wal-Mart's traditional business philosophies. The "Save money. Live better" moniker has affected Wal-Mart's business model and operations, as well as its communications. This new core philosophy highlights its responsibility beyond business to include its responsibility to society.

In the past, selling at a low price was Wal-Mart's huge competitive advantage, and it still is. But now Wal-Mart is committed to contributing to life, communities, and societies, as well as to its shareholders, its associates, the environment, and so on. Wal-Mart has embraced a global mindset, which is paying off in the business. Through environmental and social efforts, Wal-Mart has attracted a more diverse workforce, reduced significant energy costs, opened up new markets, created new and valuable product lines, and reached new customers who would have never stepped foot in a Wal-Mart store just a few years ago.

This megatransformation began with Hurricane Katrina, a natural disaster that led to a crucible experience for Lee Scott, Wal-Mart's recently retired CEO.

In 2005, Hurricane Katrina was a significant tragedy for New Orleans and the entire United States. It was also a tragedy for Wal-Mart. Over 30 of its stores were shut down, and over 10,000 of its associates displaced. Even more, Wal-Mart saw the suffering within the communities that support these associates. When the community hurts, so does the community Wal-Mart store. Many of its stores were under water. Many Wal-Mart associates lost their savings, their homes, and even their lives. Wal-Mart jumped immediately into crisis management. But this time, Wal-Mart went further. Wal-Mart donated millions of dollars and provided helpful services to thousands of people. Lee experienced Katrina firsthand as he walked through the devastation and worked side by side with Wal-Mart associates to lend a helping hand. He tells the story of Jessica Lewis, the comanager of the Waveland, Mississippi, store, who worked to help those in her community. When the flood surge swept through the local Wal-Mart store, it was a shambles. That night, though it was dark and flooded, she took a bulldozer and cleared a path into and through that store and began finding every dry item she could to give to neighbors who needed shoes, socks, food, and water. She didn't call Wal-Mart's home office and ask permission. She just did the right thing.

Lee saw Wal-Mart at its best.

And then in October 2005, Lee delivered a bold speech to Wal-Mart associates at Wal-Mart's annual kickoff meeting. Bold, because the speech was the beginning of a departure from Wal-Mart's honored "Every day low prices" practices. Below is an excerpt from that speech.

> Katrina asked this critical question, and I want to ask it of you: What would it take for Wal-Mart to be that company, at our best, all the time? What if we used our size and resources to make this country and this earth an even better place for all of us: customers, associates, our children, and generations unborn? What would that mean? Could we do it? Is this consistent with our business model? What if the very things that many people criticize us for—our size and reach—became a trusted friend and ally to all, just as it did in Katrina?

Wal-Mart is a successful business that is doing a significant amount of global good, showing love to its neighbors—increasing its community involvement, significantly reducing waste and energy produced by its stores, and building better, more pleasing stores for communities. Because of all this, Wal-Mart is genuine with its new "Live better" addition to its focus.

What Wal-Mart is learning, and others like it are learning as well, is that a self-serving pursuit of success or power undermines an ability to love others. But conversely, the willingness to love others manifests power. For the champion, power is achieved through love. For the old-style leader, power is often sought politically in spite of love. For the champion, self-serving agendas are pushed aside for the genuine win-win scenario, for the mutual benefit, for the global good.

Champions Cooperate

I believe that most people in the business world do not set out to do harm. In their minds they do what is necessary, what is practical. To call upon a common phrase, they believe they have to "look out for number one." Champions do not take this approach, and, perhaps surprisingly, they achieve practical benefits. Without delving too deeply into the realm of philosophy, let me explain.

The philosophy of egoism claims that humans are always motivated by rational self-interest and are incapable of unselfishness or cooperation. Critics of this belief reply that people perform unselfish acts every day—even to the point of self-sacrifice for the sake of others. Egoists respond that a person's ultimate motive for such perceived unselfish acts is actually a selfish desire to feel good or to gain eternal reward in the afterlife.

The philosophy of objectivism—created by Ayn Rand, a Russian-born American philosopher—takes egoism a step further, stating that the highest moral purpose in life is the pursuit of rational self-interest and happiness. Rand argues that completely mutual pursuits might even be immoral because self-sacrifice is fundamentally incompatible with the objective requirements of human life. Our only true responsibility, she says, is self-preservation.

Taking things a step further, we have Charles Darwin's natural selection philosophy, which focuses on the emergence, growth, and dominance of the fittest organisms. Organisms with the most favorable phenotypes tend to thrive, thus supporting Darwin's belief in the "survival of the fittest." Applying Darwin's theory in a social context, we are a highly competitive society in which only the strongest survive.

Whether or not they've read Rand or Darwin, some business leaders share these views. They may not feel good about hurting a competitor, but they believe it's the natural thing to do in a dog-eat-dog world, a matter of self-preservation.

Champions have a different view; one espoused—in my opinion—by, among others, Martin Nowak, the director of the Program for Evolutionary Dynamics at Harvard University. In his study "Five Rules for the Evolution of Cooperation," Nowak determines that our society's health is based upon our ability to cooperate and help each other. He uses Darwin's natural selection process to support his theory as he describes two types of organisms: dominators and cooperators. Cooperators actively contribute to each other's benefit. Dominators provide no support and are given no support by others. Dominators go it alone.

Dominators are stronger than cooperators and therefore increase in number. Over time, cooperators vanish because of natural selection. Without cooperation, natural selection favors dominators. A cooperator on its own will lose to a dominator on its own every time. Ironically, however, a community of cooperators achieves the highest level of fitness. A community of dominators occupies the lowest level. Over time, dominators struggle to survive as a species while cooperators thrive.

In other words, helping each other works better than isolating ourselves. Our research validates this finding as we found that organizational champions actively seek to support and enable close to 40 percent more people throughout their company as compared to other traditional leaders, proving that collaboration and cooperation ultimately pay out and provide a greater benefit for themselves and for the team.

Cooperation, say the scientists, relies on direct or indirect reciprocity. Direct reciprocity means I support you, you support me, and together we're better and stronger. It's a barter system and relies on repeat encounters of mutual cooperation and mutual benefit. We see direct reciprocity relationships in formal or informal strategic partnerships, in peer-to-peer accountability groups, and in open brainstorming efforts.

Indirect reciprocity, on the other hand, occurs where mutual and equal contribution and benefit don't necessarily exist. The cooperation favors one side more than the other, such as in mentor/mentee relationships or in relationships developed for charity. Repeat encounters aren't necessary for indirect reciprocity, either. For example, helping a stranger change a flat tire or a simple gesture of "after you, sir" is indirect reciprocity.

Champions are cooperators. They pursue transformational change and compelling visions by working with and through people. In fact, from the thousands of network studies SVI has launched for both champions and nonchampions, champions score significantly higher in the following network categories:

- Champions are significantly more focused on others.
- Champions are significantly more energizing to others.

- Champions are significantly more encouraging to others.
- Champions are significantly more enabling to others.
- Champions provide significantly more support and advice to others.
- Champions are significantly better problem solvers for others.
- Champions are more trusted.

Interestingly, champions were significantly more influential (outgoing influence) than nonchampions, but these same champions didn't receive any more influence (incoming influence) than did nonchampions. In other words, champions influenced others, but they weren't easily influenced by others. Others received greater relational value from a champion, whereas, the champion received less relational value. Therefore, though champions value cooperation, their desire for cooperation isn't based on the value of what they get in return. Rather, their cooperation is often indirect reciprocity because equal value or contribution might not exist.

Champions are perfectly fine with this relationship. As we saw in Chapter 3, champions don't measure their value by their networks or measure their engagement by the number of friends they have or by the amount of support they've been able to drum up. Their value is self-realized.

Building a network is far from a champion's focus. Champions aren't big glad-handers. Their relationships aren't formed to win popularity contests, but instead they are formed to produce.

So, how have they become the most effective influencers and cooperators?

Champions Pursue the Harder Right Instead of the Easier Wrong

I grabbed the statement above from Bob McDonald, Procter & Gamble's chief operating officer. Bob is an influential leader who is known for his many achievements. He attended the U.S. Military Academy at West Point, graduating with many honors and thirteenth in his class. In his military career, he became an airborne ranger and a jump master and was awarded the Meritorious Service Medal.

After the military, Bob joined P&G and quickly rose through the organization. He currently oversees all global operations in over 80 countries and all of P&G's corporate functions, such as marketing, research and development, human resources, and product supply. He's seen as a tough, no-nonsense, by-the-book leader. He is consistent, authentic, and enlightened. He knows who he is at his core, and that understanding gives him great strength. Through his self-awareness, he gets results. When you first meet Bob, you might see him as rigid, someone who isn't easily swayed, someone who doesn't struggle to do the right thing. But when you get to know him, you realize his enduring commitment to the statement from the cadet prayer he learned at West Point, "Help me pursue the harder right instead of the easier wrong."

This prayer served Bob well when P&G acquired the Gillette Company in 2005. Bob was part of the integration steering committee formed to bring the companies together effectively. Led by Bob, P&G took a "harder right" approach in the integration process. In a typical acquisition, the acquiring company absorbs the acquired, but P&G went beyond absorption, taking a "best of both" approach—another mutual-value practice by a championship company. P&G allowed itself to be vulnerable, honestly assessing its business and leadership strengths, giving the nod to Gillette when it was more qualified. When the companies merged, the Gillette oral-care president, Bruce Cleverly, was given the job of merging and running the oral-care divisions of P&G and Gillette. The message was that P&G wanted to learn from Gillette's executive talents and traditions. The move allowed Cleverly to keep the Crest and Oral B brands separate—a decision that a P&G executive would not likely have made. P&G's typical move is to combine "like" or sister products under a single brand name (i.e., Pantene shampoo and styling products). Toothpaste and toothbrushes seemed like a logical fit. By keeping them separate, however, Cleverly was able to secure more shelf space at retailers and copackage the toothpaste and toothbrush products under a smart ad slogan—"Together for a healthier smile."

In this merger of mutual value, the most qualified employees took the key positions in the combined company, regardless of whether they were from P&G or Gillette.

"Best of both" involved taking the time to understand Gillette's current practices across a wide range of areas such as marketing and manufacturing, looking at P&G's practices in the same areas, and creating the best approach by taking from both companies. Bob, and P&G for that matter, believes that this is one of the longer-term benefits of the merger—not just the talented employees and great brands, but access to all of

Gillette's best practices which have helped P&G raise its game in many areas.

Though it was a true acquisition, internally it was treated like an equal-stakes merger.

"Harder right" stories abound, and champions are behind them. In Chapter 2, I present Jim Burke, the man who was responsible for bringing Lou Gerstner to IBM. Talk about a "hard right" story. Jim ignored the conventional approach of hiring someone with a tech background and prioritized the need for someone with the right principles to move IBM forward. And it worked.

But Jim was a part of another "harder right" scenario. He was the CEO of Johnson & Johnson during the infamous Tylenol scare in 1982. Tylenol bottles had been tampered with and were filled with cyanide. Innocent people died. At the time, Tylenol owned 35 percent of the market for over-the-counter pain relief products. Following the scare, experts agreed that Tylenol was finished. But contrary to popular belief, the product found its market position again within just three years.

How so? Jim forced the "harder right," and his decision built enormous trust with consumers. Rather than downplay the crisis, Johnson & Johnson went with complete exposure, fully cooperating with the media and the public, keeping them completely informed. Rather than minimizing the financial impact of the scare, Jim forced the removal of all Tylenol bottles from every shelf and demanded that they be replaced by new, tamper-resistant packages within a matter of weeks. I remember this crisis, and, to this day, I remember how Tylenol responded. I saw a genuine champion in Jim Burke truly mourn with a nation and take the most extreme, but proper, actions.

Champions don't pursue an idea based on its ease of implementation, on the avoidance of pain, on its popularity, or on the political party line. They don't always cooperate for the sake of cooperation. Champions will occasionally transcend partisan perceptions and move forward even under the most extreme circumstances. Who shook Gorbachev's hand in Reykjavik? Arch-conservative hawk Ronald Reagan. Who signed the first legislation to seriously rein in welfare? Bleeding-heart liberal Bill Clinton. Political agendas don't clutter their vision. Champions aren't concerned with majorities—or minorities for that matter. They're not distracted by the power that groups inevitably strive to hoard. Their primary concerns aren't with crowds or teams. Their primary concerns are their love for individual human endeavor and the right thing.

Champions Champion Individuals, Not Teams

We have emphasized the love of teams over our love for the individual. We focus on team development, process, and structure over the cultivation, personal connection, and understanding of the person. Not only is building teams before individuals wrong for a person geared toward mutual benefit, but it's ineffective.

Teams aren't extraordinary; people are.

And extraordinary people make high-performance teams. By focusing more on the development of the individual, you will build a better team of individuals.

The validity of this approach was never more apparent than in the 2008 Olympics in Beijing. Michael Phelps dominated the

Olympic swimming events and has now won more gold medals than any other Olympian in history. But few of us can forget the 4-by-100 meter relay Phelps swam with his three teammates. The big story for that event was how shockingly fast Jason Lezak swam the last 50 meters of the race to edge out French rival Alain Bernard for the win. That was an extraordinary individual performance from Lezak and one of the biggest victories for team USA. This was an incredible team effort accomplished by each individual bringing his personal best. The team wasn't extraordinary—each individual was. And because of it, the team was victorious.

I understand the importance of building high-performance teams. I understand that making progress toward a compelling and worthy vision is difficult, if not impossible within a silo. I endorse culture, teamwork, healthy team dynamics, and the pursuit of team efficiency and productivity.

I'm a team guy. If I don't have a team that I can be a part of, I lose interest quickly. I love to celebrate, solve problems, and dream as a team. In fact, I teach on the subject.

I believe, however, that our focus on building teams is flawed because it's been my experience that we suppress the unique impact of the unique individual to achieve a collective agreement with equal contributions from everyone—and, ultimately, an ending where everyone feels praiseworthy. We don't want the leader to get too far out front or the follower to lag too far behind. It's everyone to the finish line with gold stars across the board.

Champions focus on individuals and their success. Underdog or favorite; dreamer or doer; winner or loser; risk-taker, maverick, or philosopher, champions aren't motivated by their potential for a following. Out of love, the champion wants her protégé to come alive. She develops his strengths not just for her own sake, but also for his sake, and through him, the team—mutual benefit (champion and protégé) and global good (team).

Of course, this approach isn't easy. Investing fully in the development of her protégé can be exhausting and can demand personal sacrifice. But it's a job that a champion refuses to outsource.

Many organizations—and their leaders—pick the easier wrong when it comes to developing their people. Organizational leaders have shipped the development responsibility to the organizational development (OD) department. Though strapped for capacity and constrained by budgets, the OD department has obliged, thereby intercepting the development conversation. In many cases, 10 people in the OD department are responsible for developing tens of thousands of employees within multi-billion-dollar companies.

This may not be how the design was intended, but I promise you that this is how the development process is carried out in most organizations. Leaders will sit in their glass-paned offices observing the faces of their 30 direct reports sitting productively at their workstations. None of the 30 direct reports dares to come to the leader's office unless dropping off a report or answering a transactional question. And the leader won't dare walk through cubicle alley—that would be too uncomfortable. No investment is made in either direction. At the first sign of a productivity challenge or a cultural issue brought about by a lack of trust, the leader places a 911 call to the nearest OD department: Help!

OD has significant value. If I didn't think so, I wouldn't be leading an organizational development company. But the value in OD needs to be in its ability to enable the organization through the growth and development of its people, not to intercept the development conversation between leaders and their direct reports. It's the champion's task to awaken the potential giant.

Champions Go Deep with a Few

Champions aren't just interested in a person's skill set. They're interested in the person, and they see mutual value in the relational connection. Champions aren't just interested in their own agenda; they're interested in the dreams, hopes, and desires of their high-potential employee, protégé, even manager. Champions know the beliefs, values, abilities, and desires of their precious few—and what makes them come alive. They also know their trials, their families, and their personal and professional limits. They give extra time to those precious few in their focus. The door is rarely, if ever, shut to them as champions give them more access than others. The access doesn't have to be some formalized, manufactured, over-burdensome relationship process. My former boss Craig never went to grab a cup of coffee by himself. He always grabbed one of his precious few to join him. Those two-minute journeys with Craig to the coffee machine were some of the most valuable meetings we ever had. I call them "fly-by" meetings. They happened often, they happened fast, and they were remarkably productive.

One of the most extraordinary leaders of the twentieth century, Jack Welch was championed early on by Reuben Gutoff, who slightly outranked him at General Electric back in 1961. Gutoff recognized Welch's value, and he knew that if GE wasn't careful, Welch would walk. Gutoff invested a lot of time in Welch and put himself on the line by promising that Welch would one day get a shot at operating the best part of the company. As an incentive for staying, Gutoff developed the idea of the small company within a big corporation, a concept that his protégé eventually took with him all the way to the top of the organization. Gutoff, it turned out, was a champion's champion.

Champions know that their investment and understanding will build real trust and loyalty, allowing them to push further and harder at times. These champions know that such personal deposits will enable bigger withdrawals down the road. But they also know that such investments are worthy and morally right.

Who are your precious few?

_____

_____

_____

For these precious few, open more of your life to them. Give them disproportionate attention, understanding, and trust, and tell them why you're elevating your relationship with them. Let these individuals be the ones you give a little more leeway to, give them more opportunities, provide greater accountability, and demand more from them because these individuals should become a part of your champions legacy.

Champions Are 100 Percent Present and Value Every Encounter

Champions understand the magnificence of the universe, and at the same time they understand the worthiness of every individual. They're less concerned about their impact on the history of the universe than they are about their impact on the people they know and love.

They have an amazing ability to exist powerfully in the moment—in the right here and right now. They are 100 percent present and laser-focused on the person directly in front of them, shutting off the rest of the world. Even though they are in constant demand, being pursued minute by minute for their advice or direction, you never see them pick up their mobile device and grab a text message in the middle of a conversation. They're incredible multitaskers, but they never let another task interrupt their investment in you as an individual.

Esther Silver-Parker is one such champion. She exudes perspective. And it's all about the perspective of what's important. Even in a massive universe, the champion understands the value of every individual and every encounter.

Esther does. She currently serves as a senior vice president at Wal-Mart and previously served as both AT&T's vice president of corporate affairs and president of the AT&T Foundation. Esther is a distinguished woman who is amazingly connected and committed to nurturing young professionals. She is one of the most transformational forces I know.

I'll never forget one amazing day in her office. The agenda for our meeting was mine, and it was all about me, my vision, and where my company, SVI, was headed. In no way was this meeting beneficial to Esther or to her professional objectives. But she had graciously blocked off 30 minutes to visit with me and provide helpful advice. During those 30 minutes, Esther received three phone calls. One from Jesse Jackson, another from Al Sharpton, and another from a U.S. Congressman whose name I didn't catch. Needless to say, these are big-time leaders of national influence. For all three calls, Esther asked her assistant to take a message because she was in a meeting. Each time, I was stunned that she continued her meeting with me that was limited in its value to her when national leaders and influencers were on the phone.

Now think about the hundreds of people you know who are constantly face down in their mobile devices, incapable of truly being in the moment. At SVI we call these people *crackberry addicts* because of their inability to depart, for even a minute, from the glow of the small phone screen or the quiet beep that says someone, anyone, wants to talk. Crackberry addicts live as short-order cooks constantly interrupted by the latest food request. Crackberry addicts are constantly allowing digital noise to interrupt even the most important meetings.

It's easy to separate the Esthers and the crackberry addicts, or the champion who is consistently 100 percent present, from the leader who is often distracted by any number of tasks. In our work, we are noticing a significant trend of the most effective leaders shifting from a *constantly available* mentality to a *fully present* behavior. This behavioral shift is improving culture in many organizations as others see, appreciate, and then adopt the value of presence. Because of it, meetings are more productive, employees feel more respected, and accountability is elevated. This concept has so greatly affected the culture of one of our clients that the client has implemented five tactical rules behind the concept:

1. Don't talk on the phone and answer e-mail—do one at a time.
2. When in a meeting, leave your mobile device at your desk or in your car—even silent rings can be a distraction.
3. Look people in the eye when you're talking with them. This includes your kids and spouse. Make a conscious choice to actively engage.
4. Don't walk away in the middle of a conversation. In other words, don't end the conversation prematurely. Make sure the people you're talking to feel they got their point across and felt they were heard.
5. If you can't actively participate in or contribute to a conversation, say so, and plan to meet at a more workable time later.

Summary

Our business challenges demand connection and cooperation within and beyond our organizations. Connection demands trust, and trust calls on a pursuit of mutual values in our relationships and through our business strategies. In times of economic and business crisis, it might seem easier to operate selfishly within a silo in hopes of beating out the others by inflating your value above theirs. It might seem easier to elevate your competitive nature within your team for the sake of protecting your turf. While such undermining pursuits might give you some short-term feeling of security, you will more surely elevate yourself by elevating your team, being a champion for a more healthy culture and through collaboration and cooperation achieve better results.

Be intentional about your relationships. Identify your precious few and initiate a greater commitment to them. Don't outsource the development and growth process, but rather personally invest in them, giving them a disproportionate amount of your time and attention.

Finally, shun the pursuit of busyness and quasiproductive activity, and embrace a mentality of being fully present in your work and in your relationships.

CHAPTER 6

CREATE ORGANIZATIONAL AGILITY

We all realize that change is constant and abundant. Our lives are lived at a faster pace than ever before in history. To keep up this pace we've become brilliant multitaskers who are able to pursue multiple ideas, have multiple thoughts, and carry on multiple conversations at once. The speed of knowledge has been fueled in large degree by the Internet. We don't date; we "speed date," conducting "chemistry" interviews in just five minutes, hoping for an immediate attraction to reward our investment in the Eight Minute Abs program.

Our pursuits can thrive one day and crumble the next. Remember Howard Dean and his infamous Dean scream in 2004? That one awkward moment zipped around the country, and his presidential hopes shattered almost overnight.

In 2008, a $700 billion economic bailout package was developed and approved within days to counter a national financial meltdown accompanied by a 40 percent drop in the stock market. The economic downtrend continues even as I write this book. Today, mergers and acquisitions strike like lightning as banks and global manufacturers set and close megadeals within a day or two because of all of this change and disruption.

We're not driving change; change is driving us—and we don't have time for organizational shock, denial, and resistance phases within the change curve. Champions are significantly better at implementing successful and complex change efforts faster than nonchampions. Organizations often crawl through change with many of their employees fighting such change tooth and nail, thereby significantly slowing the process for change and undermining its impact.

Championship companies, therefore, must be agile.

Elisabeth Kubler-Ross, a Swiss-born psychiatrist and author, studied how people deal with grief and tragedy. She identified five stages people go through in the process: denial, then anger, then bargaining, then depression, and finally acceptance. Kubler-Ross's model has been applied to how organizations and their employees deal with change as well. This application has become known as the *change curve*. It is interesting how tragedy and change can be so similar. People have difficulty dealing with them both.

This change curve, however, has been tweaked, adjusted, expanded, and simplified over time. There are many versions of the change curve today. But for now, I've taken certain adaptations to simplify and broaden its applications for our broad audience of readers. A standard change curve is shown in Figure 6.1.

Championship organizations have significantly altered the change curve to establish a competitive advantage by making themselves more agile. These organizations have created

Figure 6.1 Change Curve—Traditional Company

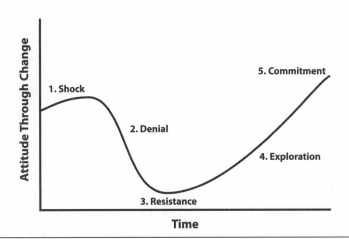

cultures that embrace change. Change has become part of their identity and is so widely accepted that people are uncomfortable being comfortable. They are constantly in exploration mode, always evaluating, always learning, and always improving. Within these agile or nimble organizations, few people, if any, are shocked by or deny change initiatives. In fact, they expect it. The "resistance"—well, they've been weeded out over time. There's no room for them in an agile company. These agile companies work under a different change curve shown in Figure 6.2.

In the early 1990s, IBM was not an agile company, as I point out in Chapter 2. It was moving dangerously close to a complete collapse because it was unable to execute a relevant business model that resonated with its customers. Within only a few short years this once dominant technology player saw mainframe revenues decline by more than 43 percent, company

---

Figure 6.2 Change Curve—Agile Company

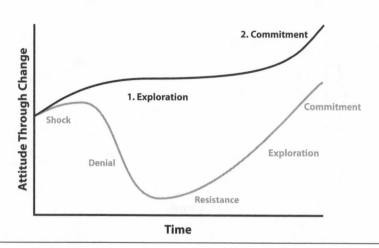

---

profits decline $800 million, and its market share plummet. Radical change was necessary.

As we discussed, when Lou Gerstner took over in 1993, he found a company that was slow to change because of its culture. As Lou made his way through IBM's managerial staff, he found the organization to be in complete denial of its grave situation. While everyone acknowledged that things were bad, people protected their own fiefdoms by spinning the message and the numbers. The denial was loud and clear: "This isn't my fault. My fairly accurate numbers show a promising story." The problem was that none of the numbers added up because many of IBM's leaders calculated within silos. An accurate financial story was practically impossible to see, and within their silos leaders made reckless assumptions about a positive outlook.

Lou focused on stopping the denial and demanded accuracy to create a complete and thorough understanding of the business. His meetings with his leaders were intense because he insisted on accurate details.

As Lou realized IBM's true position, he saw a lack of integration within the organization. He realized that IBM had the best minds and resources at work, but they weren't being deployed effectively. His move toward business integration to take advantage of the enormous resources met great resistance from many of IBM's most powerful and long-term citizens. Over time, however, these citizens either came around or were asked to leave. Once IBM acquired accurate information and eliminated the "resistance," it could begin its exploration toward becoming a healthy and thriving company again.

It's interesting to compare Lou Gerstner with IBM's current CEO, Sam Palmisano. Both are organizational champions. They are, however, significantly different in their leadership styles. IBM has benefited from both of their approaches.

According to Joel Cawley, IBM's vice president of corporate strategy, because of IBM's situation when Gerstner took over, Lou used the following approach: debate first, decide second, move third. This formula fit the challenges faced by a company lacking agility. In those times, IBM had to be very careful. It couldn't afford any missteps.

Since then, IBM has become agile. With agility come certain freedoms. It can move faster and even recover from potential missteps. Under Sam's leadership, IBM now uses a different approach: decide first, move second, debate third. IBM is smart enough to move quicker than its competition and is agile enough to land on its feet after such moves. This agility empowers the organization, and decisions are made quickly. Decisions are made, the company responds, and outcomes are evaluated for tomorrow's improvement.

This approach is lived out in IBM's client value initiative—which seems to serve as the heart and soul of today's IBM. The client value initiative—created collaboratively by clients, IBM employees, and a subset of IBM's integration and values team—puts the client front and center as every business move is made to increase the value experienced by the client. Because IBM is sensational about putting the client first, everything this company does—from its programs and measures to individual behaviors—must center completely on the value it brings. Therefore, IBM innovates for the sake of the client. IBM integrates for the sake of the client. And IBM makes decisions fast for the sake of the client in order to take advantage of the quickly evolving opportunities brought about by the unique economic times. Championed by Sam Palmisano, IBM is a *decide first* company for the value it brings to its clients.

Champions Start by Building Agility, Not by Imagining the Possibilities

It's important to note that Gerstner brought no vision to IBM when he joined the company as the CEO. He wasn't ready; nor was IBM. He snickered at the media when they asked about his vision, telling them that the bleeding must be stopped before anyone can even consider vision. Lou knew, as I point out in

Chapter 2, that many of the most compelling visions are wasted on organizations with an inability to carry them out.

Bold visions test and stretch companies and introduce new barriers. NASA's bold pursuits in space have been marred by many sputters, starts and stops, successes, and failures. Almost $600 billion has been spent on space exploration in the United States over the last 50 years and over 100 lives have been lost in the process. Some believe that over time, NASA has imagined the possibilities without establishing sound operational capabilities. With the latest space shuttle disasters, it seems that NASA is trying to have its capabilities catch up to its bold pursuits as several missions were grounded for several years following the shuttle tragedies.

In 2006, Microsoft launched Vista, its new operating system. The Vista operating system was supposed to be better equipped than its predecessors to handle music, movies, communications, and security—the very things Microsoft struggled with when compared to its competitor, Apple's Mac. Vista was a bold vision and a big push for Microsoft. However, users quickly found out that the system was slow and had low compatibility with existing software. Out of the gate, this bold vision lost steam in execution as customers became very dissatisfied quickly. After just two years, Microsoft is abandoning Vista as it speeds up Vista's replacement, Windows 7. Microsoft is agile, however, and will recover from the misstep.

Unhealthy companies have no chance for recovery from such tests, sputters, and failures. Companies with no agility will die with such bold pursuits and missteps. I'm all for imagining the possibilities; they're necessary for championship companies. But they must be countered by a company's ability to carry them out, to persevere through the trials they will bring, or to recover when such bold pursuits fail.

Champions Build Agility through Culture

Two Fortune 100 companies that we have worked with at SVI were reengineering their emerging leaders programs. The succession plans for these companies were underdeveloped because there was a shortage of capable talent to fill executive level roles within the upcoming five years. With both companies, mind you, this shortage was not the result of subpar leaders, but rather, a lack of development of the potential in these leaders. Both companies lead their particular industries, but that's where the similarities stop.

Company A is a global manufacturing company with well over 100,000 employees. The company is operations-minded and promotes a culture of inclusion and innovation. Its CEO is visibly and vocally involved in championing these efforts.

Company B has an international presence but is barely visible outside of its U.S. operations. This company of close to 20,000 employees is completely focused on and driven by the numbers. Culture and development within Company B are significant afterthoughts, but human resources (HR) talks a good game.

The employees of Company A have a sense of mission and are passionate about defeating the challenges the organization faces in the current economic environment. Despite the challenges, a cultural energy exists, along with a strong connection between the executives, the middle managers, and the frontline workers. People talk, share, and relate at all levels, across business units, and across all groups.

Company B has an independent culture with little to no collaboration across business units other than the all-too-common blame-game conversation. Financial reports aren't discussed, but rather on a good day they are highlighted and sent via interoffice mail to various departments responsible for such "crappy results." On a bad day, harsh e-mails from the top blanket all managers in the organization.

Company A delivers consistent accountability through professional and respectful conversations and methodical processes and procedures. Accountability within this organization not only protects quality standards but also demands innovative thinking and smart risk taking. In Company B, on the other hand, fear and intimidation prevail, thereby reducing innovative thinking and engagement.

Company A's CEO and executive vice president of human resources have completely unleashed and enabled its organizational development team to revolutionize its emerging leaders program along a given set of principles—tie development to the business, and fill the succession pipeline with future capable executives. The strategic development of this emerging leaders program was led by the organizational development team of Company A, but significant involvement and contributions came from several members of the executive team, from international leaders, corporate marketing, corporate affairs, its diversity and inclusion department, and representatives from each business unit. And each of these groups has been involved in all or some of the nomination, selection, development, and performance components of the program.

The entire emerging leader program of Company B was led by the training and development department, with involvement from HR but only with limited involvement from a couple of business unit leaders and no involvement from the executive team.

Company A instituted a comprehensive two-year development program that integrated business strategy with—and brought real business and social challenges to—the process. Company B's emerging leader program became more or less a one-time event.

Company A's CEO has participated in no fewer than 15 emerging leader events and meetings within a two-year period and was involved in all phases of the emerging leader development process. In addition, Company A's executive and senior leadership team has also participated in every phase of the development process. On the other side, Company B has had no involvement from its CEO, its executives, or its senior leaders.

In two years Company A has ushered 43 people through its emerging leader program and continues to have great success. The program has been touted as best-in-class inside and outside the organization.

In two years Company B has held two emerging leader events for 20 people, and the value of this program is questioned by all.

Company A's CEO continues to be a champion of the emerging leaders program, while Company B's CEO remains silent, shifting the development conversation with his most important future leaders to his training and development department.

Both these companies initiated a change to their emerging leaders programs at the same time. Company A's development program is exceedingly successful, and Company B's program is a significant bust. When you put the stories of these two companies side by side, it's easy to draw conclusions and identify the important cultural components necessary for a successful change process.

From this example we can conclude that creating an agile culture capable of driving successful change can demand:

- A cultural connection to a mission
- Connection between executives, middle managers, and frontline workers
- Cross-functional collaboration
- Accountability
- Pushing decision making down through the organization, thereby enabling and empowering others
- Commitment and perseverance through new initiatives
- Executive involvement

An organization's culture must be ready for change. A culture based on intimidation and fear of failure, where there is limited collaboration across business functions, low accountability, misaligned business strategies, and low executive involvement in change efforts, will, quite simply, fail. Champions will have to tread cautiously through such cultures, trying to drive change within the culture before change can happen elsewhere.

Change in the culture comes first for the champion. You can determine a culture's ability to change by its propensity for risk, the engagement or involvement of senior leaders, and the culture's ability to have healthy and honest dialogue in all directions—top-down, bottom-up, and side-to-side. Champions are the first to drive this dialogue. They never take someone's understanding for granted. You'll find them in many group and one-on-one discussions, taking the time to ensure that everything is understood.

For the champion, this process isn't burdensome, but rather a worthy investment of time. A champion realizes that while strategy might happen in the boardroom or among senior leadership teams, execution of such strategy is carried out by all levels within an organization. Champions have an amazing ability to hold their own at the strategy table, but then engage in open, honest, and passionate dialogue with frontline workers. They spend time out of their own offices and in the offices or workstations of others. They champion a cause or initiative through communication, by offering an honest assessment, asking for input, and presenting ideas and solutions when challenges arise. They involve many people, or stakeholders, in the change effort, engaging people from all levels, helping them understand their fit and their value to the change process.

By delegating responsibility across a broad range of people and levels, champions create organizational buy-in. Once stakeholders are at the table, champions establish roles, goals, expectations, and milestones. They identify resources and establish accountability.

Understanding the reason for change and one's role in it, along with buy-in at all levels is important because hastily considered or forced change efforts will fail. Brute-force change makers will lose to change underminers every time, even if the brute-force change maker is at the top. When change is forced, underminers dig in, even if they have to do it secretly in order to protect their jobs. These underminers might appear supportive in front of the change-forcer, but they can do lots of damage to the effort behind closed doors or through a small audience. A culture has to exist where underminers are exposed and alone, and others who fit and understand thrive. When a change effort is fully embraced by many, underminers have a hard time finding support from anyone. Healthy change requires growing support and agreement of many as it moves forward.

Champions Build Agility through Systems Thinking

When my daughter, Alex, was seven, she adored the Weather Channel. She loved it because she knew the red spot hovering over our area meant severe weather. And severe weather in our area to her meant one thing and one thing only: her chances of climbing into bed with Mom and Dad improved by 500 percent. Alex viewed weather maps through the narrow tunnel of her sweet, seven-year-old desires. She couldn't care less how or why that red smudge got over northwest Arkansas or what will happen when it goes away. She responded to a single dimension of weather: how will this affect her immediate future. That night. At bedtime. That the entire weather system would later hit Tennessee and New York meant nothing to her. That it resulted from a collision of two fronts over Amarillo meant even less. She was a single-issue kid, and when she saw that pattern, well, issue resolved. Problem solved. Make room, Mom and Dad!

Children think linearly, and it's often delightful to watch their minds work. They are singularly connected to their desires and intent on fulfilling them with major focus. But what's delightful in one moment can be exasperating in the next, which drives us to spend countless hours teaching children to think like adults.

Yet how many adults think like adults? We're supposed to outgrow linear, simplistic, childish thinking as we enter adulthood. So why don't we? What's cute and endearing in children is debilitating, irresponsible, and even dangerous in adults—especially adults charged with leading other adults. So why does linear thinking so dominate our world?

I don't know the answer, but I do know this: champions avoid linear thinking like the plague.

With every step, champions question existing modes and invent new ones. Champions are consummate learners who want to understand the bigger, broader picture and its implications. They're not satisfied with gaining two or three new insights. They want every available insight at their fingertips, and they want to see new ones flower. They don't fear people who are smarter than they are, or who know more than they do on a given topic, or who fundamentally disagree with them. They embrace such people. They want them all in the room. The work is all about the idea, not them. People buy inventions, not inventors. They understand that it's all about systems and that problems don't exist in isolation. They ask "why." A lot. And "how."

Champions have a keen eye for vestigial, linear-style, reactionary thinking, and they dismiss it out of hand.

Champions don't think stars. They think constellations, universes. They aren't just concerned about the sickness; they are concerned about all components of wellness.

Champions don't hang around for "problem solved." They're already out the door looking for "what's next." They want to know everything that might occur three to four steps beyond the remedy.

Champions hotly pursue the next "aha!" moment—especially those that will separate them, their organization, from the competition. Simply solving the problem is not their goal. Their aim is to eliminate the source of the problem and change the environment that allowed the problem to emerge.

"Problem solved" means more than "it's a wrap." It means a door just opened, a new understanding just dawned, and how do we sustain and build on it? It means, what are the new questions? It's not about ending the problem. It's about changing the ending and future outcomes.

To embrace a systems thinking mentality, champions must understand the whole of an issue or subject and its purpose or impact. But they must also understand how the whole breaks down into interrelated and interdependent pieces. It's also important to understand the natural tendencies within a system as well—how the system naturally operates, ebbs and flows.

Systems thinking as a concept has grown over the past few years. In business, I believe it has grown in large part because of customization. At SVI, it's difficult for us to pull a development product off the shelf and expect it to work for Dillard's the same way it works for VF Corporation. Dillard's and VF Corporation are two different cultures, with different objectives, in different businesses. In order for our development process or product to be successful with any client, our team needs to have a good understanding of the unique needs, the objectives, the audience, the expected business results, desired timing, budget, personalities, cultural dynamics, and so on. And we need to understand how our products can be woven in uniquely and appropriately in order to generate the best outcome and deliver the greatest value.

Systems thinking, understanding the whole and all the interdependent parts, is conducted in order to design and implement better. It's used to meet the specific needs of a specific situation through a broad and complete understanding.

Champions Build Agility through "Adaptive Capacity"

One way to recognize champions is by their resiliency despite multiple setbacks. Walt Disney went bankrupt before he realized his dream of Disneyland. Franklin D. Roosevelt became the president of the United States after he was confined to a wheelchair. Benazir Bhutto was the first female prime minister of Pakistan having had to overcome exile, imprisonment, and her own father's execution. My wife's grandfather, Pops, overcame an eighth-grade education, battles in World War II, bankruptcy, and prostate cancer, and built Airways Freight, one of the largest freight brokerage companies in the United States.

We all deal with adversity in our lives. Sometimes people fail to recover from adversity, allowing situations and challenges to determine their futures. Champions not only overcome adversity, but they become better for it.

In *Geeks and Geezers*, a book we discuss earlier, Bennis and Thomas present a new term—*adaptive capacity*. Adaptive capacity basically refers to one's ability to adapt through changes or evolutions. And according to Bennis and Thomas, adaptive capacity is quite possibly the biggest differentiator for extraordinary leadership. Adaptability gives extraordinary leaders, or champions, an ability to overcome difficult conditions and adjust their course without a downfall. Adaptive capacity enables resiliency, and resiliency is necessary for transformational change efforts, which are necessary for an agile company.

What gives these champions an ability to adapt as they continue to lead through change? What enables these individual champions, and hence, their companies, to bounce back from disruption and disaster?

The very qualities we've been discussing in this book. These champions are self-aware and therefore find self-worth and value beyond the circumstances they find themselves in. They aren't easily knocked to their knees. Because of their personal strength (enlightenment), they are perceived to be steady and poised and are given more latitude and trust to move the organization forward during transition.

These champions also have a social awareness (mutual values); they are able to influence and use their trusted relationships to help move their organization. They have empowered others and moved decision making down the ranks to enable the organization to more easily adapt during crisis. At Toyota, for example, anyone on the production line can stop production if he or she sees a problem. These line workers are empowered, and, therefore, Toyota can quickly respond, making it more agile. Red tape doesn't stop a quick solution to a problem.

According to Boyatzis, Goleman, and McKee and their primal leadership theory that I mention in Chapter 4, adaptability is a personal quality of an emotionally intelligent person. And emotionally intelligent people are as personally competent as they are self-aware and able to self-manage. These authors highlight adaptability—flexible and capable of adapting to changing situations and able to overcome obstacles—as one of five key attributes of good self-managers. They also highlight self-control, transparency, initiative, and optimism to round out self-management.

Perhaps there was never a greater crisis in modern U.S. history than the one we faced on 9/11. This crisis heavily affected the airline industry, an industry that was already struggling. But one airline seemed to maneuver through setbacks. I remember hearing the story of one of Southwest's airplanes being forced to land in Michigan by air traffic control during the ordeal. This airport had no Southwest Airlines facilities. There was no gate, no Southwest departure steps, and no Southwest luggage trucks. The pilots and attendants exited from the back of the plane and gathered the necessary equipment to get the passengers off the plane. They then grabbed all the luggage and distributed it to the passengers. Even more, the Southwest crew provided their personal cell phones so passengers could make calls to their loved ones to let them know they were safe. Some of the passengers were able to make alternative travel arrangements to get home. Others, however, obviously weren't prepared for such an ordeal and had no solutions. Members of the Southwest crew purchased train tickets for many of these stranded passengers on Southwest's dime to get them home. The crew felt empowered, without seeking approval, to take appropriate action. Because they were empowered, they were agile in the most extreme crisis, and they adapted. By the way, Southwest Airlines was the only U.S. airline to turn a profit that year.

Summary

Champions help create organizational agility. They do this by ignoring the "what's possible" right out of the gate. They recognize there will be a time for bold pursuits, but not until an agile organization is established to deal with the challenges brought on by daring moves.

Their agility efforts start with culture, building dialogue up and down in the organization, demanding accurate details, broadening stakeholder involvement, and creating alignment by helping people understand their fit and involvement.

These champions bring systems thinking to the company, ensuring that they and others understand the world of the problem, not just the linear issues.

Finally, these champions build agility by their own resiliency and adaptive capacity. They have an amazing plasticity that enables progress regardless of the obstacles.

Once an organization becomes agile, then the company is prepared to run wild and able to focus on game-changing opportunities. Agility can ignite the possibilities.

CHAPTER 7

IGNITE THE POSSIBILITIES

R ichard Branson, Virgin Group's CEO and founder, is a gravity buster—literally. So is the entire Virgin organization. The global Virgin brand is behind many compelling products from cell phones to spaceships. This brand has supported many successful product lines as well as many duds. One of its biggest successes is Virgin Mobile. In fact, Virgin's mobile business reached $1 billion in sales quicker than any other company in history—faster than Google, Amazon.com, and Microsoft. The successes give Branson and his organizations energy, while the duds fail to rein him in. Branson is an idea guy. He has an amazing curiosity, sense of wonder, and propensity for risk, and, as an organizational champion, he has the power to ignite possibilities.

John F. Kennedy was a driven world leader who also had a strong sense of wonder and a propensity for risk. On May 25, 1961, he uttered these famous words: "I believe that this nation should commit itself to achieving the goal, before this decade is out, of landing a man on the moon and returning him safely to Earth."

Those words were dangerous and exciting. Kennedy definitely wasn't playing it safe with that statement, but his words ignited a nation and the world. Following that simple yet bold statement, the race in space was taken to another level. Kennedy was already a popular president with a high approval rating. He wasn't desperate for a rebound or turnaround. He could have kept things on cruise control and still finished strong. But for Kennedy, despite the risks, there were new and promising lands and opportunities that needed to be discovered. And his competitive nature fueled his desire to be the first to the moon—ahead of the Russians.

As we all know, U.S. astronauts landed on the moon less than a decade later, and space continues to be an ongoing pursuit of many governments. Why? Because there are undiscovered opportunities out there. Possible competitive advantages exist for those willing and able to make such bold journeys. Thankfully, we aren't bound by gravity.

But the space chase has been limited to powerful governments. As I mention in the previous chapter, the United States has invested over $600 billion in its space program through NASA. While significant progress has been made, few people would call NASA's space program a complete success. Burdensome governmental infrastructure, enormous costs, and tragic outcomes have contributed to NASA's limitations.

Other governments, such as the Russian government, have experienced similar outcomes. Because of escalating costs, Russia reached out to wealthy adventure seekers to purchase a ride aboard a Russian spacecraft. Richard Branson was one of those wealthy adventure seekers. The Russians wined and dined him and even gave him special access to some of their most secret facilities. According to Branson, they made a great pitch for his business. And rightly so. After all, the price for this exclusive space journey was $30 million.

Branson had the money, and he was definitely up for the thrill. But Branson isn't just simply a reckless adventurer seeking the latest joyride. He is a compassionate man committed to doing good for society and for the planet. He's a mutual values guy who dreams big. After contemplating the $30 million price tag, he couldn't bring himself to spend so much money on himself knowing the limited value it would bring to society. The cost and the environmental consequences seemed irresponsible to him. The experience, however, sparked questions he wanted to answer:

Why is space limited to governmental pursuits?
Why can't Virgin be the first commercial galactic brand?
And why can't Virgin do it "greener"?

Branson began imagining the possibilities, and then he ignited them.

Virgin is an enterprise of the future. This global brand makes bold moves and creates organizational agility through its enterprise and partnering mentality. Having asked and contemplated his questions, Branson partnered with Burt Rutan, a well-respected scientist who had pulled way ahead of the field in the development of space technology. Together they built the SS1 and SS2 (Spaceships 1 and 2). Both crafts have successfully journeyed into space at a fraction of the cost of other space journeys with a fraction of the environmental impact. Virgin Galactic's spacecrafts are more environmentally friendly in comparison to others through its newly designed "greener" rocket engine. Because of Branson's bold moves, future space travel is within site for commercial travelers.

Virgin's agile culture of possibilities allows ideas to spread throughout the organization. Perhaps this is why Virgin is one of the fastest-growing global brands.

Few organizations have been able to create and maintain a passionate culture behind possibilities. In fact, most companies are successful at creating the suppression of passion among its workers and leaders. I call these companies *gravity companies*, operating constantly in safe orbit, unable to ignite their rockets and break through the bounds of gravity toward new opportunities.

Remember Emily, whom you met in the introduction? After college, Emily lit her rockets and started out as a gravity breaker in pursuit of a world of possibilities. After a few years with a promising organization, Emily began to succumb to fear. The company's infrastructure seized her energy, keeping her creativity bound and her ideas grounded. She shifted her focus to maintaining what is instead of pursing what's possible. She joined the organization for promise and opportunities, and she stays because of her paycheck. That is, until another company entices her with a bigger paycheck or the promise of new opportunities.

When gravity companies fail to launch pioneers through the vast and complex universe of ideas, opportunities, and possibilities, they are doomed to a mediocre existence on an aging rock of tradition—if they even manage to survive. Gravity companies suffocate in the orbital clutter and debris while their mission-minded competitors discover new worlds of ripening opportunities.

Champions Are Never Comfortable

When champions get comfortable, they get uncomfortable. Comfort leads to complacency. It's dull. It seems like, in some ways, the beginning of a slide into mediocrity. Rather than being caught in the status quo, champions constantly pursue the next big move.

When Rob DeMartini, New Balance's CEO, took over the reins of the strong but volatile brand in 2007, he began to question everything from the New Balance brand strategy to the company's treasured business partners. Observers wondered if such questions were necessary. After all, New Balance was a credible brand, a great shoe, and number two in the "running shoe" category behind Nike. But Rob knew that New Balance wasn't realizing its potential. It was losing its share of the sophisticated runner market. His next big move focused on igniting the brand into relevancy for the runner.

I knew New Balance. When I was 10 years old and living in Montgomery, Alabama, I was quite the runner. I could run 6.2 miles in less than 50 minutes—49.33 to be exact. Scrawny body and big feet made me the Forrest Gump of the neighborhood as my dad and I ran and ran and ran, in preparation for my first 10K. Up until then, my mom picked out and bought my shoes. Not anymore. I was a serious runner and was going to take responsibility for my own feet. Shoes for a serious runner are important. And for a serious runner, there was no other shoe to consider than New Balance. Even as a fifth grader I knew that. My New Balance shoes made a statement to the other runners: I was a force to be reckoned with. I wore them proudly.

But according to DeMartini, New Balance no longer acted like a significant force in the category. Instead, the brand grew stale over the last few decades in a crowded category of fierce competitors staggering under the constant push from key retailers, and from members of a leadership team with 140 years of New Balance tradition under their belts.

Times had changed; New Balance hadn't.

Rob's goal? Reignite the brand and double its growth. In his first bold move, he conducted an ad agency review, asking the company's current agency and others to pitch for the business. At the time, New Balance treasured its relationship with its ad agency. That agency had handled the New Balance business throughout the company's entire existence. The relationship was comfortable, almost sacred. Though Rob claims that the agency was perfectly capable, he felt that the relationship had become too comfortable. Neither side was pushing the other. There was little accountability either way. The New Balance brand whirled in a safe orbit, as did the agency.

Rob also determined that New Balance had become the anti-Nike—no spokesperson, limited image, more scientific than fashionable or image-oriented. Over the years, this anti-Nike strategy made it easy for consumers to understand who New Balance wasn't—Nike. According to Rob, however, young consumers who identify with a brand don't want to be told who they aren't. They want to be told who they are. The burning question Rob had to answer was who was New Balance, and what statement did its customers make by wearing the shoes? Rob wasn't looking for a campaign, but rather an idea that would reconnect the brand to its roots—the runner. After all, serious runners at one time identified themselves with and through New Balance.

The long-standing ad agency declined to pitch for the New Balance business, opening the door for other agencies to bring new ideas and fresh perspectives. And fresh perspectives they brought. Ad agency BBDO New York created the compelling and artistic love/hate TV ad, and it has completely resonated with consumers. The ad brought artistic edge and authenticity as it refused to mask the pains of getting out of your comfortable bed on a cold dark morning to lace up and run. One commercial featured a runner fighting the wake up and rubbing his eyes, only to run tirelessly through the lonely downtown streets. The image that was cast was one of a serious runner really running, sweating, and agonizing. While other brands focused on the reward, New Balance focused on the work of running and built new loyalty because of it. Runners felt like the New Balance brand really understood who they were once again.

Following the launch of the ads, message boards went nuts. Bloggers and message board writers were extremely impressed with how the brand connected a real message with real runners. No softballs, no gimmicks, no easy out. This was a bold ad for serious runners and a bold move for New Balance.

In a single act of requesting proposals from various ad agencies, Rob sent an indirect but sharp message to the rest of the New Balance organization: everyone is accountable, and everything is evaluated. As Under Armor and other growing and aggressive brands enter the category, Rob wants to unleash spirited champions who will fight for the business and defend the company's position, not traditional leaders who maintain the status quo through an established and rote infrastructure.

Bold brand moves are rare because brands are practically sanctified. But not just brands. We're often slow to adjust our ideas, processes, and pursuits. In fact, it usually takes a business or product catastrophe for us to rethink our position or our approach. Oldsmobile got old before it became "not your father's Oldsmobile." That brand got ridden to the dirt. So did Levi's, a true American icon that got comfortable and failed to relate as America changed. I could give a hundred examples here, but I'm sure you get the idea. I'm sure at some point in your career you've experienced a brand manager, process engineer, analysts, or people in various other roles who easily become more narrow-minded as their personal investment increases. They fall in love with their work—and their love blinds them to speedy consumer shifts. When someone begins to give more answers instead of asking relevant questions, you can assume that a level of comfort has set in and that learning has ceased.

Champions Squash Sacred Bunnies

In December 1991, while I was in the air force, I was assigned to attend three weeks of intense survival school training at Fairchild Air Force Base (AFB) located in Spokane, Washington. This base was strategically located near the West Coast because its primary mission was to launch B-52 bombers as fast as possible to America's primary threat at that time, the Soviet

Union. Fairchild AFB was also located in the mountains, where the cold climates mimicked those in Russia. This made it a good location to conduct survival and evasion tactics.

Several feet of snow blanketed the ground when I arrived, and temperatures consistently fell below zero at night. Survival school started with a few days of classroom training, where we were taught how to survive on our own in cold mountain climates for days and days until we were able to find our way to hypothetical "rescue zones." The training was good, and I was ready to tackle the challenge.

Before I was released into the cold mountains, I was given the standard gear and supplies that any pilot would have if he or she were forced to eject over Soviet Union territory—flares, a knife, twine, a mirror, a compass, matches, and iodine tablets. But right before I was released for my mission, I was handed one additional supply—a little white bunny rabbit tied to a leash.

When I asked about it, I was told, "No questions, Sergeant Thompson. Make sure we see you next Tuesday."

So off I trekked into the wild and cold Spokane mountain range with my supplies and my precious white bunny rabbit. The mountains were extremely lonely, especially at night. I found myself bonding with my bunny rabbit friend, whom I named Larry. I found myself talking often with Larry, though he wasn't much of a conversationalist. If you've seen the movie *Castaway*, then you know what I mean when I say that Larry became my Wilson. He didn't require too much attention. He found his own food, and I found mine—ants, bark, worms, and berries.

However, there came a point when I understood the real purpose of being given Larry at the beginning of my field training. I was starving and weak after several days of ants, bark, worms, and berries. From desperation, I looked at my precious, innocent little friend with a new objective: protein.

You see my point. We are often bound by our love for our precious little brand, our comprehensive process, or our comfortable market. And because of our love, we tend to view things myopically. We fail to see what things could be—their potential.

It's difficult to see our brands, ideas, processes, or pursuits eroding to irrelevancy because we are often emotionally and financially connected to and invested in them. They are sacred to us. Brand managers put so much energy into building it, petting it, feeding it, and protecting it that they take it personally when brand strength comes into question. Strategists painstakingly build the "perfect plan" and sometimes treat any question or suggested change as blasphemy.

Champions, however, love walking a sacred cow to slaughter, thereby, unleashing greener pastures of possibilities. They understand that if they don't, potential consequences lie ahead. They understand that hanging onto a tradition for its own sake can be catastrophic.

Rowland is a very close friend of mine who is politically savvy, heavily involved in the market, and razor sharp. I often go to him for ideas, and our discussions are always lively. We recently debated our world's current economic position and what it would take for us to rebound. It's his opinion that, as a society, we're going to have to walk a few sacred cows to slaughter.

For example, he mentioned the U.S. infrastructure. There is a vicious cycle at work here—gas needs our cars, our cars need roads, and our roads need gas (taxes). Almost every road is paid for by tax dollars. Most of those tax dollars come through the gas that we buy. So our roads need Exxon or Chevron or Mobil or Shell. And the gas companies need our roads for their customers. So does GM. If fuel consumption goes down, so will our ability to maintain our roads. If we're unable to maintain our roads, then we'll have to look for alternative means of transportation. Our fuel and auto companies will fight this to the end, and our department of transportation will too because they're obviously invested in the current system. Because of this cycle and others, almost the entire economy of the United States has been based on energy consumption.

Consumers will be forced to make the decision, and one day they will make it. Our way of life will have to be transformed, and some darling companies are going to suffer. It's not a bad thing; it's a necessary thing for progress. That's another reason agility is so important for companies. Governmental bailouts are only a short-term solution, and in my opinion, they risk prolonging a fundamental problem. A darling company's ability to survive by creating a value proposition or business model relevant to today's and tomorrow's world economy will be the thing that sustains it and gives it new life, not a government bailout package. Either you adjust, or eventually you'll be taken to slaughter.

Champions lead these charges of change. They are out in front having the real and tough discussions that they know will bring progress to our societies and to their companies. By taking an honest and accurate inventory, as they are more for progress and potential than they are for protecting their personal image or a political party, they will ensure that their companies are positioned for big rewards. They'll take their own sacred cows to slaughter in pursuit of newer and richer opportunities. I wonder if energy consumption companies, darlings of the past, are approaching the slaughter while energy producing companies are positioning for ripe rewards.

Champions Are Curious and Imaginative

Champions don't dream possibilities within their predefined role or job description. They get outside or beyond their role or job description. They don't ask for permission to wonder. They just wonder. Once they land on a true, fair, and compelling idea, a champion will embrace it. They embrace it when it's right for them, for the business, and for the world.

Imagination is a core component to dreaming possibilities. We all have an imagination. Though the psychological and cognitive science behind imagination and creativity is complex and subject to varying opinions, what's consistent is that envisioning change is imaginative, and imagination comes from the mind. Therefore, I believe some people are innately more imaginative or creative than others because of their mind's structure. This doesn't mean, however, that people who are naturally limited in their imagination and creativity are excused. According to Graham Wallas in his work *The Art of Thought*,[1] a cognitive process exists for being creative.

Whether you're naturally creative or imaginative, or you have to work for it, Wallas suggests that you prep yourself for creativity. This preparation requires a departure from the rote, reviving your mind by allowing it to wander in and out and even beyond the problem, issue, or opportunity at hand. Allow yourself to daydream a little. For some of you, this is easy. For others, it will demand the physical action of removing yourself from your typical environment before you can clear your head. Whether you can imagine at your desk or whether you require the mountaintop to see the blue sky, creative thinking requires a much broader dimension of thought than does noncreative thinking.

After preparation, Wallas suggests a period of incubation to allow broader dimensions of thought to enter into the unconscious mind. Therefore, give your ideas time to bake and evolve. Don't feel rushed to cognitively exercise the ideas in your mind's eye. At some point, depending on your creative abilities, incubation will transition to intimation and provide an unconscious feeling that a solution is at hand.

Following the intimation stage of creative thought, the idea will be illuminated and will interrupt your conscious mind. This is the eureka stage. Finally, according to Wallas, the creative thought process ends with your idea being verified, elaborated on, and then applied.

While imagination progresses within one's mind, the creative process can be valuable in a social setting as well. Often, the social setting (brainstorming) can increase the speed of an idea and broaden the dimension of thought.

If envisioning change is imaginative, creative, and often social, then the application of change calls for adding cognitive and emotional traits to the process. That's why managing change can be difficult—it's social, emotional, creative, and cognitive. And all these traits must be exercised in a change process. Most of us are stronger in one area or another, but few of us are naturally gifted within all these defined behaviors. Champions, however, are able to maximize their natural tendencies and compensate, through significant effort, for the attributes that are unnatural to them but important for the change process.

Organizational champions are able to imagine and envision such change. They can envision it because they allow their curiosity to ignite their imagination and their creativity. According to CPP, a leading global research organization and a partner to SVI, an individual with a higher than normal creative temperament makes a more successful executive. This understanding has been validated through tens of thousands of assessments launched all over the world. These executives are more imaginative, individualistic, and unconventional. They have broad interests and are seen as curious, inquisitive, clever, and resourceful. They seek variety and change and may generate original and inventive ideas.

This theory might seem unconventional, because in business we rarely reward creativity. Many of today's leaders seem to measure their worth—and are measured by others—according to the number of items on their task list. Busyness is the goal rather than prioritizing the improvement of the bottom line or the business metrics, and a sense of urgency is comfortable regardless of whether or not the task pursuits are relevant or important. Task lists are tangible and easy to monitor. Creativity and imagination are more nebulous, and harder to define. But don't let that fuzziness undermine the importance of creativity.

Champions Value Infrastructure, Not Rote Repetition

Here's where it gets tricky. It would be easy for me to bash infrastructure, to claim that a pattern of steps, processes, and communications gets in the way of our ability to imagine, to draw outside the lines, or to shift our paradigm. It would be easy for me to claim that infrastructure creates red tape and, therefore, slows down our progress and our potential. But if I made those claims, I would be wrong. Infrastructure doesn't create red tape. Culture does. Infrastructure doesn't stifle our imagination or the creative process, but rather enables it. It can make the dangerous safer; the problem manageable; the journey achievable.

Several years ago, I fulfilled my dream of piloting my own airplane. After gathering some experience in the cockpit, I decided to upgrade to a more challenging aircraft that better fit my style of flying. The Extra 300. This is not your grandfather's plane. This plane is a formula one race car with an engine twice the size of its wings. The Extra 300 was built to perform the most incredible aerobatic stunts and is capable of withstanding gravitational pressure up to 10Gs. I had no business being in this kind of plane, but I was extremely careful with it, taking many aerobatic lessons from some great pilots. I learned loops, stalls, spins, barrel rolls, hammerheads, and many other stunts commonly seen at air shows. But what surprised me as I learned these stunts was how methodical the process was for pulling them off. Performing a loop had nothing to do with a keen eye, a pilot's intuition, or casual movements of the control stick. It had everything to do with plane position, proper speed, angle of attack, rate of climb, and horizontal stability, all coordinated at the appropriate and precise time. This was no roller coaster where you hang on and enjoy the ride. Complete commitment to process was critical. A misstep meant disaster. The proper steps meant an unforgettable rush.

Process, steps, and infrastructure allow us to push new ideas, new strategies, our creativity, and our sense of adventure to the edge, methodically, carefully, responsibly. Journeying to the edge outside of a well-designed process is irresponsible at best and could be tragic.

The problem is when infrastructure paralyzes organizations by positioning process and policy over progress. Infrastructure becomes a concern when it demands rote repetition for the sake of the routine. We become a procession of elephants parading tail to trunk, tail to trunk, tail to trunk. Interestingly enough, elephants don't travel tail to trunk in the wild. We see this behavior only in the circus, where everything is micro-controlled in order for everything to be micro-predicted according to the micro-plan. African safaris are much better.

Infrastructure is necessary to define the playing field. Let's face it; the game can't be played without boundaries. Boundaries are necessary to define and maintain the game. The problem is that bad infrastructure takes over the play calling as well, diminishing the ability of the world-class athlete to execute his or her natural abilities according to his or her feel of the game. Game-changing opportunities often go unrecognized from the sidelines.

If an organization shuns infrastructure and doesn't have some semblance of consistent work processes and culture, then it lives in constant chaos with shifting direction. A company that lacks infrastructure creates a very frustrating work environment. The purpose of infrastructure, however, is to enable agility, creativity, flexibility, and efficiency. The danger is not in infrastructure or the status quo. The danger is in the passive-resistance attitude that typically entrenches itself within a gravity-pull organization that allows infrastructure and the status quo to rule.

Remember IBM under Sam Palmisano's leadership. Sam enables IBM's infrastructure for quick decisions behind compelling ideas. Richard Branson champions Virgin's infrastructure to completely support an entrepreneurial mindset. Jeff Webster takes advantage of Tyson's infrastructure and pursues new and innovative markets because of it.

Champions support, endorse, and enable solid infrastructure. They use systems, processes, and culture to maintain quality *and* drive innovation through agility and the creative process.

Summary

Today, playing it safe isn't safe. The state of business and the rise of competition, now and in the future, will demand organizational agility and infrastructure to support and enable bold and disruptive plays. These are not the days for the status quo and rote repetition. A "we've always done it this way" mindset must be replaced with an organizational creative temperament and sometimes unconventional thought.

Tradition is good and essential and is woven into the culture of every great company. Tradition tells a story and connects us to a relevant past and present. But what are those traditions that exist purely for tradition in your organization—that have no relevance or value? What are those traditions that get in the way of progress or those traditions that ignite new possibilities? What are you hanging onto purely for the sake of tradition?

How about infrastructure? Is your infrastructure enabling organizational agility and innovation or limiting it? Does your infrastructure allow your organization to *push the edge* methodically, carefully, and responsibly?

How about you? Are you comfortable floating in a safe orbit, or are you seeking new worlds of opportunity? Are you curious and imaginative, asking questions of what's possible instead of being consumed with what's typical? What charges of change are you championing?

Lot's of questions, but questions champions are continuously asking themselves and their organizations.

CHAPTER 8

WHAT YOU CAN DO TO BECOME AN ORGANIZATIONAL CHAMPION

T hus far we've studied the core principles that organizational champions live by, and we've looked at those principles in action through the stories of people who embody them in the world today. In this chapter we focus on how to apply these principles in your own situation, helping you move forward in your pursuit of becoming an organizational champion.

Chapter 3 states that organizational champions are enlightened—true to themselves, authentic, and consistent. They know who they are at their core—their beliefs and values—and they live with a strong sense of purpose.

1. Have you taken time to reflect on your own beliefs, values, abilities, and desires in order to gain a personal sense of purpose and meaning?

In Chapter 4 we cover how organizational champions personally invest and bring their emotional energy to worthy pursuits in order to inspire others. They are able to personally invest and inspire others because they have connected to—and have been moved by—savory life experiences and have embraced new levels of perspective.

2. Are you more passionate and energizing based on a true acceptance and understanding of yourself?

Chapter 5 presents how organizational champions connect with others by pushing aside selfish pursuits for the greater good. They value cooperation over domination because they know that cooperation helps them and their teams win. These organizational champions operate ethically, regardless of the political party line, forcing the harder right instead of the easier wrong.

3. Have you unleashed your passion and energy for mutual value and global good?

Then in Chapter 6 we look at how organizational champions are effective change agents who help create organizational agility through culture. These organizational champions know how to involve stakeholders, communicate across boundaries, and build support and buy-in. They embrace systematic thinking, understanding the scope of the change effort rather than focusing on a component or two. And they are resilient, able to overcome setbacks and make the necessary adjustments to see complex change efforts through to completion.

4. Are you driving worthy and transformational change efforts collaboratively and systematically?

Chapter 7 maintains that organizational champions are curious people who are able to imagine possibilities. These champions break through traditional cultures of fear and comfort to discover and ignite new and rewarding opportunities. Such transformational pursuits demand bold moves. The chapter presents how you can increase your ability to imagine more and use infrastructure to ignite your imagination.

5. Are you curious and in pursuit of new opportunities and possibilities?

These are big questions that you, and only you, must answer. For those of you who have embraced this charge attitudinally and yet have failed to make certain lifestyle changes that are necessary for such a transition, the rest of this chapter will present the lifestyle considerations of an organizational champion.

Lifestyle Change 1: Move Away from the Pursuit of Life Balance to Properly Managing Life Imbalance

A new concept has entered mainstream society over the last couple of decades: life balance. We are told by experts that we must strive to balance our lives, to be well rounded, to prioritize all the important things at all the important times. We're urged to balance family with career, personal responsibility with personal delight, spiritual growth with material prosperity. No question that this approach to life has a certain value.

But I lose interest when life balance promises control, symmetry, and predictability. A new dictatorship has formed under its guise: the dictatorship of the safe, comfortable, and secure. By developing a hyperawareness of the consequences of our actions, we've made a devil's bargain with security. It goes something like this: "Hey society, I'll give up a bold dream here, a passion there, if you guarantee me a warm bed and a peck on the cheek every night. Oh, and don't forget that condo in Boca."

Risk aversion is one thing. Denial of our own worthy desires—of what drives us—for safety's sake is another thing entirely. The complex and magnificent economic, social, and political problems of today won't be solved by passionless eight-to-five tacticians more concerned with keeping things in balance than in selling out to worthy goals.

My problem with the emphasis on life balance is the word *balance*. Balance sucks.

Literally. Striving for balance can literally suck away our passion for life, crippling our noblest aspirations by capping the energy needed to fuel them. Our goals and expectations shrink. Our focus narrows. Words like "realistic" and "adequate" sink into our vocabularies. Sooner or later, we cease to project ourselves into those territories that make us come alive.

No one's denying that life is made up of many often-conflicting parts. My beef is with the dominant paradigm for dealing with this fact. Unfortunately, in the popular imagination, life balance has become synonymous with "the right thing." But the life-balance objective is control, not risk. It is comfort, not courage. Management, not championship.

Isn't it possible that for the sake of safety and comfort—for the sake of balance—we may in fact be sacrificing what is truly right and honorable? Champions don't play it safe. Neither do the heroes we so often applaud.

Roger's Story

Roger had a lot going for him. A college senior and a starting linebacker on the Razorback football team, he had just celebrated a Cotton Bowl victory over Texas in the Longhorn's own backyard. Over 30,000 Arkansas Razorback fans roared their approval. But to Roger, only one of them mattered. He'd recently popped the big question. Amanda had said yes, and victory never smelled so sweet. "Does life ever get any better than this?" he asked as the two of them walked off the field together and dreamed of their future.

Sadly, it doesn't. Not for Roger. Over the years since that Cotton Bowl game, he's struggled to find happiness. As is common with many people like Roger, as life unfolds, well, it doesn't. It folds up. Roger's career has never fully launched, his marriage is choppy at best, and lately he's had to fight to overcome the addictions that seem to temporarily fill the gaping hole in his heart. Beer. ESPN. Internet porn. Sleep.

What happened? How could so much promise turn into so much pain? Did Roger make the wrong choices in life? Hardly. He put his family and his faith first. He showed up for all things right and all things good. He involved himself in his community, taught Sunday school, tucked his kids into bed every night. He hit his marks at work and helped out around the house. His friends and family applauded his decisions and encouraged him in his commitments. He did everything right. He put aside his own private (some might say selfish) ambition. He sacrificed achievement for a balanced life. After all, who would want to be a workaholic like his boss, an example of irresponsibility who failed to deliver on her family and community duties?

Bravo, Roger.

And why wouldn't he do just that? After all, society has pumped the balance philosophy into his head for years. The pressure is enormous to live a balanced life. To hit every base. It's colossal. The message rings clear to anyone who has come of age in contemporary society: the key to happiness is balance. Watch any random 10 commercials on TV. Image after image of Mom or Dad determined at work. Joking at the family picnic. Beaming at the kid's recital. The picture of vitality on vacation. Thoughtful at church. Generous with the neighbors. Dancing to the next chore. Hedge clipping with a smile. Tender at bedtime. And always, always healthy as sin. In every arena, utterly present and 100 percent accounted for.

What's the subtext? The underlying drill?

It's that life is a pie. It's got six or eight slices, and if you're not forking into all six or eight on a regular basis, you're letting yourself down. You're letting us all down.

But what about Roger?

Roger was made for the playing field—for the big win. He was once a spirited team player who lived for those break-out moments for himself and his team. During football season Roger understood, intuitively if not consciously, that life was no pie of six or eight slices. At most there were two: football and sleep. Well, eating, but eating was football. Classes? A necessary evil at the time, in his mind.

Amanda? She was the bright light waiting at the end of November, when the season ended.

After he graduated—easy enough too, because he knew when to hit the academics—he caught on fast. He looked around and realized that no matter what the speechwriters say, life is not football and football is not life.

So, from one playing field to another (this one had walls and a computer), Roger resisted the temptation to work past five o'clock, claiming that it cut into family time. Fair enough. He resisted job-related travel because he had regular duties at church, and he hated to miss even a single Saturday morning at home. He shrank back from his so-called career responsibilities because he knew better. He saw that his responsibilities were split six ways and work was just one. His job was a means to a paycheck, not an avenue to pursue his passion.

What was his passion anyway? He'd slipped into a set of values—he didn't know when it happened—that left him feeling guilty anytime he missed supper. His performance at work suffered despite continuous encouragement, advice, and pleas from his boss. But he certainly wasn't going to be one of those career-driven drudges who, like his boss, failed to deliver on his responsibilities to family and community. Besides, hadn't he helped reduce supplier contract fees by 0.08 percent in a mere 18 months?

So Roger got fired. After a nonproductive stay with one employer, he was forced to find another job. He hadn't seen it coming. Confidence shot, spirits down, he accepted a role with another company that held less meaning for him. Forget passion. Roger needed to earn some cash and put food on the table. It became a matter of basic survival. In those occasional spare moments when Roger had time to lift his head and look around at his world, he wondered why he hadn't been rewarded for pursuing a balanced life.

How quickly we can lose it—our passion and zeal—any one of us.

Here lies the life-balance myth. Parceling out limited resources equitably across multiple responsibilities is pretty much impossible to do and is certain to underdeliver in the long run. The right approach is not about sharing energy across an array of priorities. It's about selling out to them one by one or, at the most, two by two. As I write this book, my priorities are writing, my family, and my company—SVI. I've hardly exercised over the past four months. I've put on hold many relationships with friends, and my Sundays will one day involve going to church again. But not now. Don't get me wrong, my faith, friends, and fitness are extraordinarily important to me. But for this four-month period in my life, I'd be paying lip service to them for the sake of perception and a verbal pat on the back. I would hear, "How do you do it, Mike?" and know full well that I don't. I can look really balanced and really good at accomplishing next to nothing. Priorities—things we like, things we want to succeed at, even righteous obligations—need full room to breathe. Pursuing balance as a principle means slowly lowering the oxygen levels of the things that are most important—with a smile.

Roger halfheartedly directed his emotional and physical resources, everything he had, into his pursuit of a better-balanced agenda. Consequently, his family, his circle of friends, his church and community, and even his vacations and personal pursuits became duties rather than fulfilling arenas of activity. He found little joy and even less achievement in anything he did. His performance was mediocre across the board, and nothing—nothing—was extraordinary.

Ironically, the same friends and family who once encouraged him and admired his values began to regard him as irresponsible, unskilled, and unwilling to work hard.

Society talks a good game, but society is fickle. It encourages personal fulfillment through a balanced life of apportioned responsibility. But what does it reward?

Look around. Martin Luther King Jr., Ronald Reagan, Helen Keller, Jonas Salk, Arnold Palmer, Sandra Day O'Connor—make your own list. These people, these champions, moved our world, lifted our consciences, broke new barriers, not by worrying themselves through day after day of carefully allocated responsibility. Society rewards the single-minded passionate pursuit of an overriding purpose. Society rewards missionary zeal. Maybe society should learn to talk what it walks.

6. Are you pursuing life balance or properly managing life imbalance?

Lifestyle Change 2: Live Passionately and Securely

Roger's story—a fictionalized composite of three or four clients we've known over the years—may seem extreme. But it's all too common. We've seen it played out hundreds of times in our work with all levels of management. Key elements in Roger's story come up again and again, centering chiefly on the sheer frustration that comes from chasing an impossible ideal: the mythical balanced life that exists only in TV commercials. A misplaced sense of security or responsibility tends to over-shadow every aspect of life. Passion gets the leftovers. That's if there are any leftovers, and usually there aren't.

It may seem that I'm beating up on the whole idea of security and responsibility in life. I'm not. Instead, my target is the tendency for security and responsibility to choke off passion. I contend that many of our struggles in life—with depression, anxiety, or addiction, with inertia, with our inability to champion—stem from the pressure to subordinate true desire to a more socially accepted lifestyle of "suitable" balance across multiple responsibilities. Roger's failed pursuit of that lifestyle sucked away his passion for life. He embraced the lie that society fed him, and it took a devastating toll on his family and his future. I'd argue that the toll was felt by society as well. We missed out on Roger's potential. He was far from the champion who'd stood on the 50-yard line at the Cotton Bowl Stadium.

It doesn't have to be that way. Being secure, responsible, and passionate aren't mutually exclusive. They can all coexist.

Look at the continuum below. At one end, security. Words like safety, responsibility, commitment, duty, role, and consistency should come to mind. At the other end, passion. Associated words: energy, action, excitement, intensity. Even love.

Where would you put yourself on the continuum? Which set of words characterizes your life the most?

Upon honest reflection, you might put yourself somewhere along the left half of the line. This would hardly be unusual since, in contemporary life, the pursuit of security does tend to shoulder out passion. And while there's certainly no right or wrong answer (the key phrase is "honest reflection," the more honest the better), I believe passion is both undervalued and undercultivated in our society while being a key ingredient in overall happiness, emotional health, and progress. So, depending upon how far to the left you put yourself, it's my feeling that some degree of change might be beneficial, if not downright necessary, if you truly aspire to be an organizational champion.

For those of you who planted yourself somewhere along the right half of the continuum—evidence that there's a healthy quota of passion in your life—stay with the discussion.

Something else happens at the far right end of the spectrum when passion, unfettered by responsibility, is allowed to run completely amok, leaving a trail of relationship debris in its path. If you find yourself way out there, changes may also need to be considered.

Others of you will have resisted pinning yourself to one point on the continuum, feeling, quite rightly, that at any given moment we're actually in flux, shifting left or right. Let's focus on that feeling.

Try this. Pick two points on the continuum, one that represents you at your most responsible and the other, at your most passionate. The space between the two points represents your own personal continuum within the continuum. Your personal zone. Next question: within that zone, where do you spend the most time?

Take this process a step further by plotting a zone for each of the various sectors of your life, say, home, family, career, recreation, church. Again, within each of these subzones, where do you spend the most time? At the security end or the passion end?

I'm not a huge fan of charts and multiple-choice or fill-in-the-blank personal assessment surveys, but I am supportive of the need to take a good, frank look at what's operating in your life. So don't fuss too much with the exact placement of these endpoints, but do throw something down. Chances are you'll stumble across some degree of insight, even an aha moment or two. Better yet, for a surprising dose of perspective, ask a trusted friend, colleague, or family member to do the same for you. I believe strongly that the best authority on you is you; still, seeing yourself through another's eyes is bound to provide further insight.

Look for patterns. Is passion the key player in any one of your zones, or does security dominate across the board? Does your career zone include much passion? How about your home life? Intense passion in one zone can sometimes make up for a high degree of security in another. On the other hand, little passion anywhere could signal trouble. Little or no passion in the zone where you spend the bulk of your time (probably at work) might surely be a problem or, as I'd prefer to think, an opportunity.

Again, there is no correct set of answers, no proper way to run your life. We're all different. Nevertheless, there can be little doubt that champions share one thing in common, and that's passion and energy. The good news is that nothing in life is static and that adjustments, however incremental, are entirely possible. We can, in fact, regulate our individual relationship with the two ends of the continuum.

A champion consciously and deliberately maneuvers back and forth along the continuum between security and passion. This is contingent upon timing, need, and opportunity. Sometimes champions will need to give full rein to passion and deprioritize security. Other times champions will forsake passion for security. By consciously positioning themselves at various points along the full breadth of the continuum, no endeavor—whether infused with passion or security—need ever descend to mediocrity. Each task and each experience receives maximum attention at the appropriate time, rather than the distracted, half-focused attention that comes with having one eye on the life-balance meter.

What you hope not to see are these two hypothetical individuals:

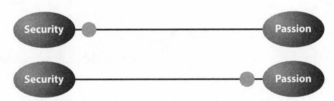

The continuum plot for a champion will look more like this:

Again, at certain times champions will completely immerse themselves in their passion. Then there will be periods when their chief concern will be managing their responsibilities for the sake of security. They identify beforehand when and where those times are, those critical times when they must be at their peak. They work both ends of the continuum in all aspects of their life—and they are intentional about it.

My Wife, Mel

There exist a few fortunate souls whose passion and security, duty, or responsibility are all the same. Like my wife, Mel. Mel's chief responsibility lies with the security of our kids, Alex and Jax. Her true passion? Alex and Jax. No dilemma, no vacillation between passion and security. No personal struggle in that department.

I can be passionate about our kids too. I love them so much that it hurts. When I'm away, I miss their laugh, their eyes, and our intense wrestling matches on the bed. They are a significant source of joy and comfort for me. And I feel enormously responsible for them and their security and well-being. But they are not my passion-filled dreams. At times, I'm completely immersed in my mission, and my kids take a backseat. Other times, my mission takes a backseat, and I'm completely immersed in my kids. Here's the point: in neither instance do I split my attention in a vain attempt to balance family and career at the same time. I no more desire to be a mediocre father than I do a mediocre executive. I go all out for my business: speaking, traveling, writing, pulling late-nighters to meet a deadline, even missing dinner. Then I take Alex on a father-daughter ski trip in Park City, or spend the day watching movies with my wife, or shop in Seaside, Florida, with my family, or visit the Miami Boat Show with my friends with my iPhone off.

"I Love My Family, but They Don't Drive Me"

Bob Basten, past CEO of Centerprise Advisors, was dying of Lou Gehrig's disease (ALS). Knowing he had little time left, he nevertheless worked until it was no longer possible—first at the office, then from home, setting up a nonprofit foundation supporting ALS research.

Announcing his resignation from Centerprise, he shed tears in front of his executive board. "I'm crying here," he said, "and I didn't even cry when I told my family," according to an article in *Fast Company* by Christine Canabou titled "Never, Ever Quit." He had poured his heart into Centerprise Advisors. It consumed him. And the company had been a tremendous success: with $170 million in annual revenues at the time of Bob's departure, Centerprise Advisors ranked 15th on the list of the top 100 accounting companies.

I bring up Bob because of the fascinating editorial exchange and reader response that stemmed from that *Fast Company* article. At one point in the story Bob is quoted in a heresy: "I love my family, but they don't drive me." This honest admission—true of any number of men and women who are passionate about their work, their art, their mission in life—brought a hailstorm of outrage. Here's just one response:

> As I read your story on Bob Basten, I felt my emotions grow. Not at his disease, which is a horrible thing and unfair for anyone. My shock and dismay were at the complete imbalance in his life. He cried when he announced his pending death at the board meeting but not when he announced it to his family. I'm

also disappointed that *Fast Company* portrays him as a leader's leader. It is disgusting to see how little Basten cares about his family in your story. When he can't dress himself, will his stockholders help him? No, his family will. Ten years from now, will the board visit his grave site? No, his family will.

There's at least one glaring fallacy in this response, and that's the assumption that Bob cares little for his family. If you read the article (and I highly recommend it), there's nothing to suggest that Bob's family life is anything other than tight, loving, and fulfilling for all concerned. Another fallacy concerns the ultimate impact of Bob's life. Sure, the Centerprise board members likely won't be spending time at Bob's grave site. But will they and thousands of others continue to feel the positive impact of what Bob accomplished in his life? You bet they will.

The response to the Bob Basten article reflects the subtle, but profound, influence of the life-balance myth in society—the assumption that a given quantity of family time has a certain inestimable value. A value that, by definition, will always be greater than time spent away from family.

Am I suggesting that you set up a permanent cot at work? Not at all: the moment your passionate pursuit of a mission becomes an excuse for ducking family life—for not taking care of business at home or in some other sphere of responsibility—we part company. What I am saying is this: discovering and aligning yourself with an objective that you feel strongly about is at least as important as fulfilling the responsibilities you inherit as a member of society. Because, to return to Howard Thurman once again, what the world needs most is people who have come alive.

Let's jump to an extreme example of responsibility versus mission.

Secret Service Special Agent Tim McCarthy wasn't even supposed to be assigned to the president's detail on March 30, 1981. But that afternoon, thanks to a fateful coin toss, he found himself lying face down on a Washington, D.C., sidewalk with a .22 caliber bullet lodged in his stomach—a bullet intended for President Ronald Reagan. Unlike everyone else in sight who hit the pavement, McCarthy "made himself large," intentionally shielding Reagan.

The bullet that entered McCarthy's right chest would almost certainly have found the president—that's a celebrated fact. Uncelebrated is the fact that Tim McCarthy had a wife at home and two children ages two and four. Would anyone question McCarthy's action on the grounds that he cared little for his family? The special agent loved his job; he was passionate about serving his president and his country. He did what he was trained to do with no regard for his responsibility as a father—he took a bullet for the president. Would it occur to anyone to accuse him of being a neglectful father in that instant? When McCarthy visited Reagan in the hospital where they both recovered, he had his two kids with him. What would they have felt, years later, if their father hadn't made it?

Again, an extreme example. But I use it to make a point. Responsibility is relative. Dedication to mission does not preclude dedication to family and security. Nor does dedication to family preclude dedication to mission.

Plan your peak performances when they count, regardless of whether or not those performance periods are categorized as pursuits of security and responsibility, or passions, or both.

Know when to work, when to challenge, when to disconnect or reconnect, when to play, when to rest, and when to serve.

Understand that passion and security need not be in conflict; rather, know when to submit to the dictates of your passion and when to partake fully and joyfully in the comforts and securities of life and in your responsibilities.

Remember that we're not responsible only to the people we love; we're responsible to our passions in life.

7. Are you living extraordinarily in all aspects of life—giving full rein at appropriate times to your passions and to your responsibilities for security?

Lifestyle Change 3: Become 100 Percent Present in Everything

We discuss the idea of being 100 percent present in Chapter 5 as it relates to seeking mutual value. Being 100 percent present in your relationships makes you a better listener, builds trust, and increases the productivity or value of the relationship—mutually. I'd like to expand on this idea a little and elevate its significance.

The younger generations are sometimes described as the MTV generation—constantly seeking quick bursts of information and entertainment. Attention spans are narrowing. It took days for my grandfather to grow bored with an activity, it took a day for my father, hours for me, and it seems like seconds for my kids.

At the same time, the number of tasks that we might manage at any given time continues to grow. I noticed my wife's to-do list earlier this week. It's Thursday, and she's already got four pages of things to do, with another four pages with tasks scratched through. As business leaders, we're seemingly doing more, juggling lots of pieces at once. We've reached the multitasking revolution. And by the way, I think I'm pretty good at it as I write this book while listening to music from Coldplay.

But more and more scientists are confirming that while we might be increasing our ability to multitask, this work method is still less productive than intensely focusing on a single task. In fact, studies show that multitasking reduces our satisfaction and our productivity, and it increases our stress. Constantly shifting mental focus might help us process more things, but at the sacrifice of having little understanding for what we've processed or why we've processed it. Jonathan Spira, Basex's CEO and chief analyst, calculates the business costs of multitasking to be over $650 billion annually in lost productivity. In the first century BC, the Roman slave Publilius Syrus once said, "To do two things at once is to do neither."

Multitasking is hard to escape in today's environment. Often it might even be necessary. Champions, however, seem to operate more within a concept that I call fast-tasking, in which they give full rein and intense focus to one task, rapidly shortening the time it takes to complete it. These champions might appear to be multitaskers because of the enormous workload they are maneuvering through. But in fact, they are 100 percent present on each task, giving their physical, emotional, and intellectual capacity completely to one area of focus. And we all see the benefit from the quality and efficiency of their work.

You know these people. They are prepared for every meeting, they aren't distracted, and they seem to contribute to anything they are involved in. Never are they casual bystanders.

For years I was perplexed by such people. How could these extraordinary leaders, consummate strategists, and micro-analysts with global responsibilities, hundred-million-dollar budgets, and crazy travel schedules function so well in their enormous roles? How do they appear so calm and organized? How do they have time to invite me into their office and look me straight in the eye, listening intently and giving great advice in the midst of abundant demands coming from the ring of the phone or the ding on the computer? They are fast-taskers—100 percent present in every moment that is worthy or worthwhile to them and to you. Not everything is of interest to organizational champions; they don't hesitate to say no to the things that aren't.

As you consider adopting certain lifestyles of an organizational champion, consider moving from being a multitasker to a fast-tasker. Be 100 percent present in everything you do, intentionally blocking outside distractions. Take an interest in every encounter. With every task, commit to intense focus and efficiency—even speed. Set a new pace for your work and elevate your level of contribution by being 100 percent present, interested, and involved.

8. Are you 100 percent present in your pursuits and in your relationships? If not, how can you move closer to that goal?

Lifestyle Change 4: Recharge Your Battery

Radical Sabbatical is one of SVI's most highly rated development programs. The name itself is a little oxymoronic—sabbaticals are often more restful than radical. But the oxymoron is intentional because the program itself has some oxymoronic components. Radical Sabbatical is an intense and experiential development program that currently takes place in Costa Rica. The objective of the program is to help executives escape their greatest challenges and their treasured luxuries in order to discover the world and themselves and become better global leaders. Costa Rica provides an ideal setting for this personal journey. Over a period of five days these executives are pushed emotionally, physically, intellectually, and spiritually. It is a remarkably productive time for growth and awareness. But it is also a wonderful time to breathe, to wonder, to see, and to take in some of the richest and most rewarding views that life has to offer. The Costa Rican rain forests help these executives get mentally lost enough to truly disconnect and find themselves. They rest and recharge.

People don't recharge enough. Many of the most successful leaders reach peak performance quicker than others, outpacing their peers. They work extremely hard, perform well, fail to properly manage life imbalance, and burn out fast—if not at work, then at home.

Living a champion's life isn't easy. There are easier pursuits, no question. Champions put their lives out there for others, for mission, for performance, for possibilities, and they thrive in demanding times because of it. Because they thrive, others track and shadow them, constantly tapping into their energy and seeking their insights. It doesn't take long to drain champions' batteries, as they personally invest and sacrifice themselves for the sake of others.

Therefore, it's critical that champions recharge their batteries often. Recharging isn't just healthy; it's productive. Properly managing peak performance and rest is how the eastern block countries dominated the Olympics in the 1960s and 1970s. Their athletes trained differently from the way athletes in other countries trained. While most countries were training to achieve peak performance and maintain peak performance throughout the games, the Soviet Union categorized its training in periods of peak performance and in periods of rest—a strategy called periodization training. Figure 8.1 shows the differences in the training regimens.

Notice how traditional training has a difficult time increasing peak performance, while periodization training methodically grows peak performance. Additionally, more athletes get burnt out and injured in traditional training than do athletes who participate in periodization training. Periodization is the common training regimen for most high-performance and professional athletes today.

Organizational champions know how to manage rest and peak intervals too. They know when their batteries are low and when they need to recharge. These champions know that if they don't recharge, they'll fail to improve. Champions will give everything to a project or a team but will follow it up quickly with solid rest and recovery. They know the value of a sabbatical for lengthy recharging. They enjoy vacations for midyear recharging. They know when to take a day off and when to take a brief walk to the water cooler. They manage peak and

Figure 8.1 Differences in Training Regimens

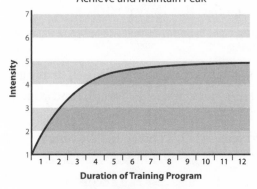

Traditional Training Programs
Achieve and Maintain Peak

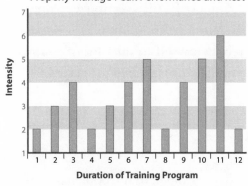

Periodization Training
Properly Manage Peak Performance and Rest

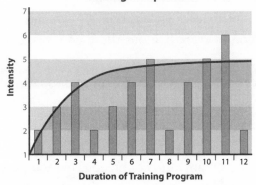

Training Comparisons

rest intervals in their life, throughout their year, their month, and during their day. Recovery is necessary for the performance of a champion.

9. Are you intentionally taking time to recharge throughout your day, your week, your month, and your year?

A point to remember: When you take time to recharge, make sure you achieve your rest and recovery objectives. Sometimes family vacations are not rest and recovery. I'm all for running with my kids on the beach, but I can be fairly worn out when I return from an intense family vacation with my nine- and three-year-old. I, therefore, commonly take at least one vacation a year completely by myself to do a lot of reading, sleep in, eat good meals, and take on an adventure or two.

Summary

Up until this chapter, much of the book has focused on the core principles of a champion—what a champion does.

This chapter focuses on lifestyle adjustments that will better enable you to truly live out these core principles—how a champion does it.

How does a champion do it? Champions manage life imbalance by giving full rein to various and noble pursuits at appropriate times, never fractioning off their energy for all of the perceived "good things" at once. They live passionate lives, ignited by their dreams and courageous in their pursuits. They are fast-trackers, not necessarily multitaskers, and are able to focus intensely and contribute to everything they selectively involve themselves in. Finally, these champions know when and how to recharge. They can outwork most, because they know how to bring in rest and recovery to their lives.

Part III of this book focuses on how you can manage and develop champions and benefit from their results and impact—why champions do what they do and why championship companies embrace these organizational champions.

THE PROMISE OF THE ORGANIZATIONAL CHAMPION

CHAPTER 9

UNLEASHING THE ORGANIZATIONAL CHAMPION

U p to this point in this book, we discuss the nature of organizational champions and how you can develop the qualities and the approach to become one. In this chapter we take a slightly different perspective, namely, why you develop champions and how to manage them.

It might be an accurate assumption that managers would appreciate the impact of a champion or champions on their team—passionate change-makers developing exciting ideas. However, cultivating champions and managing them require a greater commitment than simply overseeing transactional staffers who put in their time, meet their deadlines, and tend to their task lists.

Champions don't respond to the usual management techniques. People with drive toward possibilities come alive in spite of fear or intimidation, certainly not because of it. With their strong sense of a greater purpose, they are not seeking the immediate gratification of a pat on the back. Typical staffers can be managed in traditional ways because they are passively waiting for life, waiting for their moment, waiting for retirement, promotion, inspiration, or a kick in the pants. Or worse, they've given up altogether on their pursuits of meaning and potential.

Champions know what they are passionate about, and they know how to integrate their purpose with their organizational responsibility. They find extreme satisfaction in their work because they are able to align their core identity with what they do. Their work matters to them in the grandest sense.

More than ever, organizations need people who come alive, who are aligning their personal passions or their sense of mission with the needs of the organization. As we discuss throughout the book, the complexity of the business and social climates today demands a higher and bolder commitment and aptitude.

Champions will happily ally themselves with organizations and organizational processes and systems that they believe in, but they'll never allow themselves to be defined by them. Instead, they are more likely to define or redefine processes based on what's possible. They define themselves by their own mettle.

Organizational champions think less about following procedures within a role and more about their potential to have an impact on a business and on a society. Even as champions smile and nod in a job interview, they're thinking, "How can I have an impact on this company, this organization, this world?" Once onboard, these champions are able to sustain their drive and not succumb to the organizational politics. They are less motivated by "smileys," good reviews, and incremental pay raises than they are by their own vision, their belief in the shared vision, and the continuing opportunity to test their own mettle through relentless pursuits of possibilities. They'll endure pain if they sense that they're having an impact or, quite literally, leaving a dent on the organization. Organizational champions are resilient, but the one thing they won't compromise—or compromise for long—is their sense of their own potential, not for mere compliance with the system.

Some managers might conclude that organizational champions are in it only for themselves, and to a certain extent that's true; they do expect to win. But don't misinterpret a strong drive toward what's possible with selfish ambition. Quite the contrary. It's not a race for the biggest, baddest social network or the biggest personal prize. A champion's drive is for win-win scenarios and for possibilities that are mutually beneficial.

In fact, they love teamwork—but not for its own sake. They love teamwork because they find it stimulating, personally fulfilling, and efficient. They see it as often the shortest distance between two points on the way to fulfilling their vision, or the vision they share in. Champions will happily work with others, but again only if they're regularly able to test and build on their personal strengths and invest in the personal strengths of other individuals on the team.

To the degree that you have identified your needs as their manager, these mission-minded people will find ways to engage in it; but they can be tough to manage if you're not sure how to do so. Champions like to run ahead and drive change. They seem to be constant learners. The best will run ahead of you. Are you okay with that? If you understand what's at work, you should be. Managing champions means giving them the opportunities to succeed even in the toughest challenges and keeping them engaged. It means understanding them personally as well as professionally. It means being a champion yourself. The truth is that I have yet to come across a single role leader, one who leads by the task and only through his or her job description, who could effectively lead a champion. Role leaders might easily become frustrated by a champion they are responsible for leading.

Why? Because role leaders often think myopically, while champions embrace the contribution from a diverse team of passionate and capable people. Role leaders will often try to unintentionally or intentionally limit the impact of champions, keeping them reined in, controlled, and managed tightly. They might refuse to unleash the champion for fear of their own personal or professional consequences, such as losing credit for a good idea, catching the flak for a failed but bold pursuit, or losing control of their comfortable and safe management silo. Role leaders will hang onto the hierarchy and manipulate the politics for the sake of personal status in place of progress. For role leaders, their position is first. They will protect it at all costs. For champions, progress is first.

Before I come across as too harsh toward role leaders, I need to express that I do have sympathy for them. Naturally, managing organizational champions is difficult. They'll challenge you, sometimes even expose you to your own weaknesses. They don't always respond to the same stimuli as process-oriented team members. They question, sometimes when there's no time for questions. They might not always have the right answers, but they certainly know the right questions to ask. They want to understand the premise for various organizational actions and how they can best connect and contribute.

With that said, how do you handle such people, such champions? How do you take advantage of their enormous potential? The rest of this chapter addresses these questions.

Value Their Uniqueness and the Organization's Diversity

Earlier I reference Tom Marshall's book *Understanding Leadership* and introduce a term that I love: McLeaders. Marshall uses the term to describe the process by which many organizations cultivate new leaders. You'll recognize the premise: a promising individual, X, is identified within the organization. Once selected, Mr. or Ms. X steps aboard the organizational leadership conveyor belt. This same conveyor belt created and spit out organizational leaders A through W, and the same conveyor belt will create and spit out organizational leaders Y, Z, AA, BB, CC, ad infinitum. McLeaders, one and all.

"X, Y, and Z are just the kind of leaders we need in this organization. They get it. They know what's expected, and they fit in well with the other leaders."

The McLeader story, though not related, is illustrated well in a book I recently picked up titled *The Peacock in the Land of the Penguins* by B. J. Gallagher Hateley and Warren H. Schmidt. In the book, penguins do a great job of leading—so long as nothing changes and adjustments aren't necessary. They value the same limited skill sets and follow the same decision-making formulas. When a peacock pays them a visit one day, the penguins don't know what to make of it. The peacock claims to be interested in the penguins and their penguin organization. The peacock even wants to join their leadership team. The penguins are intrigued but, hmm, a little wary. They soon realize that the peacock doesn't get their leadership style. This bird is bringing different ideas and a different style to their leadership team. And they don't like it. They want the new bird to talk and behave like a penguin. They know what works and think that everything is perfectly fine as it is.

Deep down—if we're honest with ourselves—don't we all often find ourselves operating under the penguin principle: if it ain't broke, don't fix it? It's penguin nature, after all. Protect it.

You know where this is going. The penguins remain blind to the value of the peacock because the peacock doesn't lead the way they do, doesn't display the same skills, and doesn't always make the same decisions. But you'll have to read the story to find out how the saga ends.

Again: champions value diversity—and not just diversity of thought and ideas. Champions know that the best ideas come from a collection of people of diverse styles, experiences, backgrounds, attributes, and interests. Collaboration and sharing between diverse groups of people are necessary for the progress of products and services in today's global marketplace. When such diversity exists, the right ideas for global opportunities are on the horizon.

The disabled have influenced pay-at-the-pump technology. Women have influenced the production of new wines and beers with fewer calories. Latinos have filled our grocery stores with great new salsas. And we've all benefited.

The value of diversity is obvious for the champion, but it doesn't stop there. The champion just plainly enjoys working in a colorful and multidimensional environment.

Champions themselves are diverse, sometimes operating under different personal or professional objectives and often walking to the beat of their own drum. You can't put their leadership in a box, and you shouldn't try. They lead through a vast array of styles. Their diversity is often the source of their breakthroughs.

As you champion champions, your objective should be as much about their agenda as it is about yours. Your approach should value their style as much as you value yours. Seek to understand them through open dialogue and genuine interest. Share your thoughts openly and honestly and let them know that agreement is far from necessary with you, that you're interested in progress, the best ideas, the championships, not blind consensus that suppresses opportunities.

Align Them Personally to Your Organizational Mission

Champions don't accept jobs. They accept missions. A job description on a sheet of paper is just a starting point for them, the basics, the lowest common denominator. While job descriptions effectively present the duties, responsibilities, and requirements, I've never seen a job description that presents the "what if—wow" potential. Champions effectively carry out, but aren't limited by, the job description. Their work and impact are felt way beyond it.

The job description helps to determine fit and alignment, and it provides a basic understanding of expectations, but it is developed entirely from a particular job function or role.

The same document accommodates any number of people within the defined role. One job description presents the duties, responsibilities, and requirements for national sales managers, all one thousand of them.

Many of these descriptions focus solely on the role and fail to form a connection to the individual and that individual's potential. The job description might protect you from a lawsuit as it establishes and aligns an agreeable basis for performance, but it might do very little to cast a compelling vision or ignite a champion's interest.

To maximize the impact of champions, you must move beyond qualifying them for the role and onto connecting them to a mission that they can personally embrace. In order to connect them, you must know your mission or purpose well and connect with it yourself.

Northrop Grumman does. Though it hires its designers based on strict guidelines and qualifications, this global defense and technology enterprise accompanies the strict qualifications with an exciting presentation of its mission and purpose as being the future of aerospace and defense. It casts a bold vision and compelling mission for potential hires and builds their excitement beyond the role. These designers are offered the job because of their qualifications, but if they are champions, they accept the job because they personally connect to the mission.

Disney often ranks at the top in many listings regarding the best places to work. It doesn't hire for roles. It hires the best people that fit perfectly into its mission. It's all about one's creativity and the ability to create the magic, the dream—Disney's mission. At Disney, the qualification for working is simple: can you make the magic happen? And the company's cast members do it very well.

Marriott International begins its courtship of potential hires with the statement, "You've found a place where you define what success means to you, and we help make it happen." Marriott understands that hiring the best means connecting to and enabling an employee's dreams.

I'm a U.S. Air Force guy, but if you compare airforce.com with goarmy.com at the time of this writing, you'll find a very different approach to connecting people with roles. The army does it better. The army's Web site builds its brand by telling the gripping story of a candidate's potential in the army. You can't help but be intrigued by this community of soldiers. The air force, on the other hand, tells no such story on its Web site, but rather presents a static picture of a girl in uniform next to job roles divided into three categories—enlisted opportunities, officer opportunities, health-care opportunities. The air force connects people to the jobs; the army connects people to the dreams.

An interesting book by Matthew Kelly, *The Dream Manager*, calls on companies to counter a lack of engagement and turnover by making a personal commitment to understanding and even enabling the dreams of its employees. P&G's Bob McDonald strongly supports this idea. He knows the desires and dreams of his employees, and he encourages the idea of enabling dreams throughout the P&G culture. This is a new mindset and approach for many, but the idea seems to ring true through most competitive organizations like Marriott, the U.S. Army, Disney, Northrop Grumman, and P&G.

These companies understand that there is nothing more powerful than enabling one's personal dreams under the umbrella of a compelling organizational mission. A good place to start is by changing your interview presentations and questions for a potential new hire. If the hiring process begins with the interested candidate signing in and then waiting in a small lobby full of fake plants and gimmicky art, consider an adjustment. If the interested candidate is later greeted by human resources and other stakeholders who then proceed to ask the hundred best standard interview questions, consider an alternative. If, somehow, the interested candidate accepts your offer, and your final words are, "We're glad you're here. Good luck," consider a modification.

Instead, get the marketing and HR people working closer together to create an emotional attraction and connection with the candidate. Make sure that your message and mission are understood and compelling enough to catch the emotions of star performers and woo them. Don't start with qualifications. Start by identifying hopes, dreams, and ideas. Start by telling your brand story and cast the vision of possibilities. There will always be room to review qualifications.

But this is just the beginning. Make sure your interest doesn't diminish after the acceptance. Remaining connected with your top performers keeps you from talking a great game, only to fail on the delivery of expectations and ultimately crushing trust. Today, tools such as e-mail, corporate intranet communities, discussion groups, text messaging, and social network technologies are all acceptable relationship-building tools or processes that allow even the busiest people to invest in each other efficiently and frequently. Don't limit your relational involvement to just these tools, but prioritize your relationships and use your cultural tools to remain connected. Participate and engage in existing programs such as high-potential development programs or business resource groups. Executive involvement, access, and personal interest are the biggest differentiators in thriving cultures. Make sure, with your best people, that you remain connected and that you know the following:

- What they are good at.
- What makes them come alive.
- How they uniquely contribute to the needs and mission of the organization.
- How the organization uniquely contributes to their needs and dreams.

As an organizational leader, you can't afford to treat your best performers as cogs. Champions can be complex individuals. They are multidimensional. When they invest in missions they find worthy, they invest their whole lives. If you're fortunate enough to find people who align personally with your organization's purpose, then they deserve your understanding of their whole self.

Give Champions Disproportionate Amounts of Your Time and Attention

Have an open door policy with champions. But don't settle there. Establish a walk-up policy as well. Don't wait for them to come to you. Go to them. Those champions who have championed me in the past didn't wait for me to schedule time with them. They initiated it—and often. The fact that their office had a couch and my cubicle had only one chair (mine!) didn't keep them from pulling up their own chair or kneeling on the carpet.

One of my previous bosses in particular, Craig, whom I mentioned before, demanded my time at 5 a.m. every morning for a lengthy run regardless of rain, sleet, snow, or hail. These runs were often physically painful, but they were professionally productive for me. Because of his investment in me and the investment from others, I connected and grew. I was committed to Craig, the team, and our business, and he made sure that I knew how I fit within the organization and that I knew my value.

The obvious question is where do you find the necessary time to invest? As an organizational leader, or champion, there are few openings in your schedule. What I've found, however, is that the most successful executives prioritize this time. Few things are of greater importance to them than investing time in their most important assets—their top talent.

There's no question that such an investment must be limited to the stellar few. Spreading yourself too thin across too many relationships is detrimental to your culture, to your productivity, and to your own ability to recover. SVI's research confirms that organizational champions represent approximately 20 percent of a leadership team. As a general rule, if you have a leadership team of 20 people, 4 of them are potentially champions. They need your disproportionate focus. These are the ones who are the most productive, the most inspirational and influential, and the most effective change agents.

But is 20 percent the right population of champions on your leadership team? Not every leader in an organization needs to be a champion to create an agile culture capable of thriving in today's business environment. Many of the executives we interviewed were less concerned with the percentage of champions and more concerned with having enough champions to seed their organization's culture with core principles. Their prescribed rule of thumb is to have enough champions at all levels in the organization to encourage cohesive risk and force change, transformational activity, and organizational agility.

Demand a Lot

Much of this chapter might seem to be about giving the organizational champion an easy ride, a soft pitch, or an open pass. I'm not endorsing protective behavior at all—quite the opposite, as you'll soon see. It is, however, important to communicate the necessity of your personal investment in an organizational champion. Your investment is all about making enough deposits in the relationship in order for you to make some massive withdrawals. Ask relationship experts, and they'll tell you that you'll get out of a relationship what you put into it. You're making an investment disproportionately in champions because you're going to demand disproportionately more from them.

Many organizations are facing their toughest times, and many are in desperate need of extraordinary leaders—champions. Now is not the time to coddle or protect them, but to deploy them in the harshest environments. It's time for them to lead complex turnarounds. Put them on your best opportunities or your biggest crises.

Why?

Because they're the best at dealing with these kinds of things.

Complex projects demand a high degree of trust, capability, and sensitivity. Champions are able to build trust and are concerned and sensitive listeners who can execute effectively with poise. They deserve to be in the ring with the lions. Kim Partoll of AOL is in the ring with AOL's Access business. The young Bill Dillard III is also in the ring, as he's been assigned to turnaround Dillard's once dominant cosmetics category.

The story at PepsiCo is Indra Nooyi. She's a champion who rose to the top spot at Pepsi in 2006. But before being promoted to CEO, she was a corporate daredevil involved in the most visible, significant, and fragile projects. Indra championed the dumping of some of PepsiCo's most sacred brands like Taco Bell, KFC, and Pizza Hut. She led the acquisition of Tropicana and the merger with Quaker Oats in 1998. These projects and assignments were the best of the best and the worst of the worst assignments. These were assignments made for champions.

According to *BusinessWeek*, since Nooyi become involved as a chief executive at PepsiCo, the company's annual revenues have risen by 72 percent, while net profit more than doubled, to $5.6 billion in 2006. Many believe that PepsiCo's significant revenue and profitability growth are because of Indra's bold moves and championship efforts. Who can argue? She was on the toughest stuff that made the biggest impact.

But when you ask her about the people who disproportionately invested in her, this daredevil grows soft. She's got a long list and describes each of them gratefully. From the late Wayne Calloway to the most recent previous CEO, Steve Reinemund; Indra describes how so many people not only inspired her, but coached her through the good and trying times. She gives full credit to their guidance. These leaders and mentors invested much in Indra and expected much from her—and PepsiCo is being rewarded because of it. So is Indra.

Establish Accountability for the Outcomes, Not the Outputs

Under even the best circumstances, you don't really manage champions. You unleash them to their own devices. Their best work might happen when you're out of the room. You unleash them to journey and discover. You unleash them to win, sometimes on their own, for the benefit of many. You unleash them to make their own impact for the benefit of the organization. You unleash them because, if you don't, you lose them. You lose their promise and their potential. And they lose their opportunity. Failure to unleash a qualified champion is a lose-lose scenario.

You unleash them by establishing the boundaries and then giving them space. You unleash them by managing the results, not the tasks and by holding them accountable for the outcomes, not the outputs.

We discuss earlier how Tyson Foods unleashed Jeff Webster to take Tyson's by-products and turn them into more profitable bio fuels. In pursuit of this opportunity, Jeff Webster is calling the plays for his team. He is managing every detail, making timely adjustments, coaching his people, analyzing the competition, and capturing creative ideas. However, Tyson's executive team defined the playing field and established the boundaries—no new costs and no messes.

Lee Scott, Wal-Mart's recently retired CEO, unleashed Andy Ruben to champion grassroots environmental sustainability efforts across its entire business and turn sustainability into a competitive advantage. However, Scott defined the playing field and established the boundaries—deliver systemwide execution and make sure it pays off financially.

Ken Barnett, CEO of Mars, unleashed Rob Rivenburgh to build a high-performance culture behind a bold and transformational vision. However, Ken Barnett defined the playing field and established the boundaries—the process must improve and not burden operational efficiency, and the results must be measurable.

Richard Branson, Virgin's CEO, unleashes hundreds of corporate entrepreneurs to start up new start-ups. Richard's boundaries—make it fun and make sure it builds the Virgin brand.

In all these cases, we find how champions of champions established the boundaries and allowed their protégés to call the plays. These organizational leaders and champions of champions monitored the score—the outcomes—and invested in and organized the people. They understood the passions and capabilities of their protégés and how their passions and interests aligned with the needs and opportunities of their organization.

Once they aligned them and provided the right focus with the right opportunity within a given set of parameters, they could then monitor the outcomes and not concern themselves with the outputs. The vast majority of the battle, as we've likely often heard, is getting the right people, in the right places, pursuing the right things.

Before leaving this chapter, it's important to give attention to ways a champion can *manage up* to his or her supervisor or manager who might not be an organizational champion. When a champion doesn't have the necessary authority, a champion might consider the following actions in order to influence the culture and advance the organization. Besides, these recommended actions are important for all champions regardless of your circumstances, but they are especially true for a champion with limited authority.

Be Prepared

Champions must know the business better than others. Because their supervisors or others on their team might have a low propensity for risk, these champions must be well researched and able to call upon case studies in order to support their causes. A champion's push for change needs to connect to expected results, and as often as possible, include a return on investment calculation. With limited authority and managed by a traditional leader, a champion cannot rely on creative brainstorming, conceptual debate, or casual but progressive conversations. These champions must be fully prepared for the challenge in order to be successful in the debate.

Communicate Often

Communications from a champion to a role leader should take place often, both formally and informally. Formal communications are sometimes necessary in order to ensure two-way dialogue that might not happen casually. I find the best results happen when the conversation is set up by champions stating their desired objectives of the conversation and the key points they'd like to make. I recall a recent conversation I had with an individual. Our previous conversations had often been unproductive and one-sided—his side. I needed to get my points across to him, but not come across as too aggressive because he'd surely shut me down or take the conversation over. I began by saying in 30 seconds exactly what I hoped the conversation would accomplish and the key points I'd like to present. I then told him to take all the time he wanted to share anything on his mind, but I need three complete minutes of uninterrupted time to present my case at the end. He took advantage of his opportunity to talk, but then he gave me my three in the end. The ten-minute conversation was our most productive ever, and I got exactly what I needed. The formality of the conversation pushed him to honor my requests, and it pushed me to be prepared with my speaking points and be efficient and on target. We've both agreed to conduct such formal conversations on a weekly basis since we both now find them valuable.

Not all your conversations with a role leader, however, need to be formal. Make time for informal conversations as well in order to build the relationship and allow each of you to get to know each other better, beyond the job. These conversations should spur understanding and trust. I'd encourage these casual conversations to be quick check-ins, rather than deep debates of world politics. I call these quick conversations, *fly-bys* in Chapter 5. They are short, casual, and great relationship builders that can happen often.

Invest Personally

You might not get much in return initially because there is rarely a short-term payoff for such a relational investment from a champion to a role leader. But over time, your personal investment in your supervisor will payoff. Your supervisor wants to be known, understood, respected, and appreciated. And chances are your supervisor has a great respect for you even if it's seldom shown. Remember, role leaders are rarely vulnerable; they play things close to the vest. But don't let that stop you. You have a different agenda—to be unleashed. The only way you'll be unleashed is if you can gain massive trust. Therefore, you must invest—making personal and professional deposits so that you can withdraw from relational funds when they count most. Just as I encouraged you to *discover yourself* in Chapter 3, you should discover your supervisors, understanding who they are, what they are good at, what makes them come alive, and how they uniquely contribute. You should encourage them in their growth and acknowledge their successes. Be their champion.

Stretch Opportunities

When championship opportunities open up, don't double-check for approval. Run full speed ahead. You likely have a small window of opportunity as your role leader might not be fully comfortable with a bold pursuit you're tracking. Push right up to the boundaries in order to fully take advantage of the opportunity and maximize its impact and reach. A hesitant approach to a bold pursuit will deliver subpar results and harm future opportunities.

General Chuck Yeager is arguably the most famous test pilot of all time. He made his mark on the history of aviation by being the first pilot to fly faster than the speed of sound. In 1947, Yeager was assigned to test the rocket-powered X-1 fighter plane and potentially break the sound barrier. It wasn't known whether a winged aircraft could fly faster than sound—or, if it could, whether it would hold together. Nor was it known whether the human body could survive such an ordeal. Yeager broke the sound barrier on October 14, 1947, mere days after cracking two of his ribs in a horseback riding accident. I'm a pilot, my father was a lifelong military pilot, and my brother piloted combat missions over Iraq in the F-15. We know the rules. Many people consider chasing the sound barrier with a pair of cracked ribs outside the rules. It's definitely pushing right up to the edge of them. But Yeager knew what was at stake for aviation and for his own career, and he didn't care about procedure for procedure's sake—not with stakes like that staring him in the face. Chuck Yeager was, to say the least, a handful to manage. He was also the first living creature to travel faster than the speed of sound.

That's what test pilots do. That's what champions do. They stick to a plan as long as they can, but when the plan falters—out there at the edge of the envelope—they're ready. When others won't move, or can't, champions do. They don't fly blind, but they also don't wait for a perfect sky. When the opportunity presents itself, they jump into action.

Chuck Yeager did that. He thrived outside the envelope, and millions came alive through him for what he accomplished.

Revel in Small Victories

It might be rare, initially, for game-changing, transformational opportunities to present themselves under the guise of a role leader. Therefore, it's important to remain engaged by celebrating the small victories. Every good salesperson celebrates an invitation to pitch after fighting through the many number of "no's" they receive. There are countless stories of how prisoners of war celebrated even the smallest victories, such as solving a math problem in the dirt or establishing any level of contact with their comrades in order to remain sane. I acknowledge that such circumstances are incomprehensible and incomparable to the business setting, but the point remains. Celebrating the small victories will give you energy and drive so that you will remain and persevere until the small victories lead to some big opportunities.

Such celebrations will help you remain positive and optimistic despite setbacks. Our research shows that optimism is a common trait for champions. Their optimism serves them and others well because they become the example of a desirable culture—and others follow. An optimistic culture keeps people engaged. They end up spending less time in frustration and more time in working proactively toward organizational solutions.

Place This Book on Your Role Leader's Desk

WINK!

Summary

As you assess your readiness to champion a champion of your own, ask yourself the following questions:

- Have I identified my organizational champions?
- If so, have I embraced their unique style and value?
- Have I aligned them personally with the needs and mission of my organization?
- Am I giving them disproportionate amounts of my attention?
- Am I demanding a lot from them, putting them in the most challenging arenas?
- Have I established the boundaries, and am I monitoring the outcomes more than the outputs?

As you assess your ability as a champion to manage up to a role leader or supervisor, ask yourself the following questions:

- Am I well researched, prepared, and equipped to communicate my plans and ideas based solely on forecasted business results?
- Am I formalizing my communications with my supervisor to ensure that I have adequate time to thoroughly explain my idea and get feedback?

- Am I discovering my supervisor, investing time getting to know her beyond her role, learning her habits and desires?
- Am I taking advantage of my opportunities and pushing the boundaries of an assignment in order to maximize my impact?
- Am I acknowledging and even celebrating small victories?

CHAPTER **10**

WHAT ORGANIZATIONAL CHAMPIONS DO FOR YOUR COMPANY

I've been in the business world for almost 20 years, and based on what I've experienced, heard, and read, I can honestly say that there has never been a more exciting time for business. The economics at work in the twenty-first century create continually evolving opportunities behind constant unpredictability as the rapidly growing numbers of sophisticated consumers around the globe flex their buying-power muscle. Innovations and countless niches are emerging from all directions as the number of technology-enabled producers grows. Lower barriers to entry for these producers combine with an abundance of consumer choices from a fast growing middle class to create a dynamic and competitive global marketplace. Everyone has a voice, and the marketing buzz is now generated more from the roots and less from Madison Avenue.

There are no more "one-size-fits-all" scenarios or domestically led international initiatives. Ideas come from around the globe and are deployed according to specific, varying, and finicky consumer needs and interests.

Add to this whirl of energy the increasing noise coming from a planet that is becoming more crowded and hot, and no one can ignore the significance of the times. Businesses face a growing number of social challenges, and everything is in flux. So you can choose to be really scared or really excited. Very few knowledgeable business leaders are bored.

The most agile companies, the ones that make bold plays and focus on mutual and global value, will win the most in today's global marketplace. And, as we've discussed, organizational champions create these companies. The rest of this chapter presents how champions enable agility, ignite the pursuit of possibilities, and build global trust within championship companies.

Champions Build Global Brand Trust

Because champions are enlightened, authentic, and consistent, they inspire trust. They are significantly more trusted by others than are nonchampions. These champions have been seen going through the fire and recovering, even excelling. Challenges haven't changed them, nor has corporate or competitive pressure. These champions have an amazing ability to remain steady and poised despite the crisis or the crucible.

Though champions have their favorites, they are fair. No one can question their integrity as they're consistent in their accountability, regardless of who you are. As mentioned earlier, they don't operate for political power but for progress. Even if you don't like them, you respect them.

But what does the ability of champions to earn trust have to do with their impact on global brand trust? First, allow me to affirm what I mean by "global brand trust." I don't mean "global" in the sense of "worldwide." I'm referring, instead, to a complete application of trust. Champions aren't trusted only by the majority; the minority trusts them too. Champions aren't trusted only by their own teams; other teams trust them as well, even competing teams. Champions aren't trusted only by one customer segment; they're trusted by all customer segments. But if the champion's trust stopped there, then trust would live and die with the champion. That's not the case.

Champions aren't just trusted; they create trusted teams and trust in and between teammates, trusted products and services, trusted strategies and innovations. As a result, the worldwide brands they create are trusted by consumers. Brad, our local Starbucks drive-thru cashier in Fayetteville, Arkansas, built trust with my wife by ensuring a consistent Starbucks experience. He created that trust by knowing my wife's name, our children's names, our anniversary date, and her very complex coffee order. In essence, Brad built my wife's trust in the Starbucks brand. She's extremely loyal—it's a whole morning experience for her as it is for millions of people, likely because of a good product delivered by thousands of respectful, considerate, and consistent Brads. Brad has since moved on, but my wife's trust in the Starbucks brand lives on in large part because of him.

Champions are able to grow cultures of trust. These cultures of trust affect both a company's internal brand among employees and a company's external brand among consumers and partners. This cultural trust is built through systemwide collaboration, a pursuit of mutual values, and a champion's consistent and visible personal commitment.

These brilliant collaborators never assume they have all the answers. They love it when the line between "my idea" and "your idea" blurs and everyone benefits. As risk takers, they know how to mitigate risk, thereby building trust, by seeking insight and input from others. And they understand that it's only through collaboration that inspiration develops exponentially, yielding the strongest ideas. It's rare that their collaboration has a limit. Champions like to involve many as long as the conversations are efficient and productive. Part of the collaboration process is to serve up and confirm the idea, and part of the collaboration is to establish buy-in among all stakeholders and align culturally behind the idea. Such collaboration helps identify potential pitfalls by allowing various individuals, teams, partners, and customers to express their concerns in order to arrive at a workable solution that is mutually or wholly beneficial. A one-sided scenario can lead to a win-lose scenario, something that would jeopardize trust for the champion, the team, the customer, and the organization. For the champion, the conversation continues until mutual or global value is established. This is obviously often a harder and lengthier process. But as *Built to Last* authors Jim Collins and Jerry Porras state, there's tyranny in the *or* pursuit and genius in the pursuit of the *and*—your good *and* my good.[1]

These champions are great examples for teams, cultures, customers, and partners because they demand global (overall) collaboration until global (overall) benefit is achieved.

Stakeholders observe the fact that these champions likely have an easier way to see an initiative through. But champions will never take the shortcut toward execution at the expense of trust. It goes against their personal values. Champions will remain personally involved and invested until, as Bob McDonald of P&G puts it, the harder right is achieved instead of the easier wrong.

Champions Establish an Industry Edge

Lou Gerstner of IBM was ahead of the technology industry curve. Though he was mired in the details of IBM's operations, he was keenly aware of a slowly progressing market shift that none of his competitors had realized. And he bet the farm on it.

In Lou's words taken from his book *Who Says Elephants Can't Dance?*, the bet was that, "Over the next decade, customers would increasingly value companies that could provide solutions—solutions that integrated technology from various suppliers and, more importantly, integrated technology into the processes of an enterprise." Simply put, Lou was banking on software and systems taking a backseat to services and solutions.

Lou was almost a decade ahead of twenty-first century economics—niche players meeting specific consumer demands. He anticipated that thousands of niche players would continue to drive significant growth within the technology industry. But there was no one established as the integrator of all of this growth and market fragmentation. If IBM could secure the integrator position through services and solutions, then it would have tremendous influence over the industry and capture its leadership position once again. Lou's hunch paid off. Solutions and services became IBM's edge and helped it rise to the top.

We'll have to wait and see if, a decade from now, Richard Branson's bold and courageous race to space establishes Virgin's edge in a new and exciting industry—commercial space travel. Gerstner and Branson have made bold and courageous moves. One has already succeeded, and I'm pulling for the other one to pay out as well.

Such bold or disruptive moves are nothing new for champions. They are necessary in order to differentiate their brands from the competition and establish an industry leadership position—even creating entirely new industries.

My company, SVI, in partnership with Rockfish Interactive, is banking on our collaborative and flexible online training platform, named Genofish.com, to differentiate us from traditional learning management system business models. Our Web technology and innovative user interface differentiates us from our competition and brings innovations to the online training industry. Time will tell if this technology gives us the edge in this competitive arena. I'm betting on it.

Champions who make bold plays to help their company differentiate and establish an edge in their industry search constantly for new ways to compete. They look for breakthrough opportunities based on anticipated needs. They don't wait for market maturity or fate, but rather take fate into their own hands by remaining on the offensive.

This is not an easy process for champions or their organizations. Such bold moves might be at odds with established business practices and tradition, thus creating organization tension. Therefore, bold moves that create a competitive edge must be made without doing harm to the established business. Special attention must be given to protect business as usual while business as possible is developed.

Champions look far and wide for ideas that can provide an industry edge. The book *Blue Ocean Strategy*, by W. Chan Kim and Renée Mauborgne, explores how an industry edge can be formed through the creation or discovery of new markets. The authors examine the difference between red oceans (an existing and crowded space where cutthroat rivals exhaustively compete for incremental growth) and blue oceans (untapped markets that are ripe for rapid growth). A blue ocean generates new market demand, while competitors in a red ocean battle back and forth within existing demand.

One case in point the authors present is Yellow Tail wine, from Casella Wines in Australia. It's the fastest-growing foreign wine label in U.S. history, becoming the number one imported wine within just three years. To create such amazing growth, the winery looked outside the $20 billion wine industry and investigated the beer and spirits industries to form its market strategies. From its research, Yellow Tail built a blue ocean strategy, avoiding the typical pretentious and intimidating position of wine for the sophisticated drinker. Instead, it followed the beer and spirits industry—simplifying its label, making the brand fun, and positioning its wine as an everyday enjoyment.

Yellow Tail uncovered an entirely new way to compete with, and rise above, its competitors. This company looked way beyond its industry to build its edge—typical of a championship organization.

Champions Create Competitive Advantages

Identifying ways to build a competitive edge through bold, game-changing pursuits requires vision, imagination, and curiosity. It requires lots of "what if" questions and a keen anticipation of future needs through knowledge. But then the question becomes, how do you turn those bold, disruptive pursuits into competitive advantages?

There are hundreds of examples of bold moves falling flat and even leading to failure. Monsanto, a chemical company that has strived for an edge through biologically engineered food since the late 1990s, has been unable to turn the pursuit into a company advantage. This bold idea sounded promising, at first, as an ingenious way to counter the decline of natural systems while population and consumption accelerated. But Monsanto underestimated the worldwide resistance to genetically modified crops, which was especially strong because of Monsanto's checkered history of harming people and the environment. The company that wanted to genetically engineer our food was the same company that created Agent Orange and NutraSweet. Monsanto had neither the trust nor support to turn its idea into an advantage, a failure that forced then CEO Robert Shapiro to step down. Monsanto remains committed today, however, and it will be interesting to see if this bet eventually pays off.

Many other companies have suffered similar fates out of the gate. Bold moves are just that, bold, in part because they involve risk. At the same time, standing still can be just as risky—even more risky. But first-to-market doesn't mean first-to-win. Think of all the first-to-market ideas that ultimately lost their market share to latecomers. How did Kodak, the original inventor of the digital camera, allow Cannon to take the lead in the digital camera industry? How did Rio MP3 lose to Apple's iPod? How did Netscape get beaten by Microsoft Explorer? Being first doesn't necessarily mean "winner." Gaining an advantage through an edge means being first and then executing your position effectively to sustain dominance.

Making a bold and industry-disruptive move is only part of the story. Such moves are usually internal quests conducted by those who are keenly aware of an organization's core—its principles and strengths and weaknesses, its identity, its customers' needs. If we examine bold moves that fail, we can see that one of the reasons for failure often involves misunderstanding that core identity.

To manage the risk involved with bold and disruptive moves—as well as to create advantages such as increased speed to market, reduced costs, and global best practices—championship companies are forming collaborative relationships that give them more options and nimbleness without forcing enormous investments or battling stifling red tape or infrastructure.

Championship companies have switched from a "go it solo" approach to a highly collaborative process of multiple organizations. Many progressive CEOs have learned to collaborate through an enterprise business model to survive. Purely internal innovation—identifying, developing, and executing new ideas from within—is no longer cost effective. Championship companies will grow more partnerships—even with competitors—to build good, cheap, and fast competitive advantages.

Sam's Club and fierce competitor Costco have collaborated to create more energy efficient retail clubs. Sam's Club then CEO, Doug McMillon, invited Costco executives to tour Sam's Club's newest energy-efficient club. He exposed the new heating and air system that contributed to significant energy savings for the sake of improving the industry and the environment.

Champions are the ones who are championing the efforts. They are building advantages by building trusted relationships across entire development and supply chain systems. These champions are building advantages by forcing global value that keeps all organizations and stakeholders involved and engaged. These champions are building these advantages through their ability to communicate well across boundaries and even influence across cultures with people they have no real authority over.

Turning a bold idea into a competitive advantage is simply a complex change process, and champions are extraordinary agents for change because they know how to involve others and establish buy-in across entire internal and external systems.

Champions Create Growth and Value

More consumers are experiencing greater prosperity as the middle class around the world grows. At the same time, technology has enabled the significant growth in the number of producers of products and services. Growing consumer needs served by a growing number of producers are creating a global economy of abundance rather than an economy driven by the hits, according to Chris Anderson, author of *The Long Tail*. I'm describing *hits* as those consumer-driven must-have products. In 1983, the Cabbage Patch doll was a *hit* toy that was in such great demand that these dolls caused riots around large retailers. Michael Jackson's *Thriller* album was a *hit* as it set new sales records and won seven Grammy Awards. Harry Potter the movie was a *hit* and became the highest grossing film series of all time.

Today's economic model is shifting from an economy driven by the hits to an economy driven by an abundance of choices. I might like the band U2, but I now have the choice to access less popular bands such as Postal Service and Scissors for Lefty, an electronic indie-pop band. Today, distribution is just as easy for the lesser known bands as it is for U2. And the costs to me are the same—99 cents per song. I'm no longer limited to just the hits, but I have an abundance of choices that I can access that are perfectly suited for me.

In *The Long Tail* Anderson points to the Internet as the provider of so many new choices. For instance, compare the music selection on Rhapsody to the number of choices at your local music store. And more choices are accommodating more tastes. This economy has opened its doors to a huge number of niches as scarcity wanes. We are now in a postscarcity economy. Add growing consumer knowledge to the new economic rules, and it's easy to see why product or service innovation has never been more important.

Companies are having a harder time keeping up with the speed of demand for the new and the better. We still love our hits. There's just a lot more of them today, and few of them have significant lasting power in the market. Products and services often grow stale as the mature phase of the lifecycle begins a lot sooner than it did in the past. Not long ago, innovations that occurred every five years were standard. Today, global companies introduce a number of innovations within a single year. These companies are looking everywhere for these innovations, and partnerships are helping to decrease the gap between customer demand and an organization's ability to meet the demand.

Behind these strong partnerships you'll find champions who not only imagine the possibilities and create agility, but they drive innovation engines that contribute to exponential growth opportunities. Today, these innovative engines are fueled by partnerships with customers, competitors, suppliers, universities, and governments.

Our SVI team has worked with the Washington Regional Medical System for a few years, and together we've developed some amazing new products for the health-care industry. Bill Bradley, Washington Regional's CEO, has always been open to our team beta testing ideas with his organization. Washington Regional gets the benefit of lower costs and slightly customized solutions faster than competing hospitals get them. Through our partnership we've created a new online employee satisfaction survey specific to the health-care industry. The new survey costs less than half the price of the previous survey, and it is much more efficient, capturing more than twice the compliance rate. It's cheaper, faster, better. Our innovation in partnership with our client has opened a whole new market for our product.

Procter & Gamble, always ahead of the pack, wants to innovate with everyone. It will review any idea from anywhere as long as the idea is connected to an innovator with a patent, a trademark, or a product for a potential transaction. P&G

has even branded its innovation process; it's called "Connect + Develop." This open innovation strategy has its own Web site (pgconnectdevelop.com) through which anyone can submit a product idea. Gil Cloyd, P&G's recently retired chief technology officer, offers the statement below in support of Connect + Develop:

> It's our version of open innovation: the practice of accessing externally developed intellectual property in your own business and allowing your internally developed assets and know-how to be used by others. Historically, P&G relied on internal capabilities and those of a network of trusted suppliers to invent, develop, and deliver new products and services to the market. We did not actively seek to connect with potential external partners. Similarly, the P&G products, technologies, and know-how we developed were used almost solely for the manufacture and sale of P&G's core products. Beyond this, we seldom licensed them to other companies. Times have changed, and the world is more connected. In the areas in which we do business, there are millions of scientists, engineers, and other companies globally. Why not collaborate with them? We now embrace open innovation.[2]

Today, open innovation at P&G works both ways—inbound and outbound—and encompasses everything from trademarks to packaging, marketing models to engineering, and business services to design. It's much more than technology.

Through open innovation, P&G has launched hundreds of new products over the past few years. A small French company partnered with P&G to provide the active ingredients in what became Olay Regenerist, a significant product line within the $2 billion Olay brand. An independent inventor from Canada partnered with P&G to create the first dryer-added softener, Bounce. One of P&G's competitors from Japan partnered with P&G to launch Swiffer Dusters in various markets around the world. In addition to P&G more than doubling its new and innovative product launches through partnerships, R&D productivity at P&G has significantly improved, and innovation costs have fallen.

Champions realize that innovation is not a department, but rather an open pursuit of ideas. And innovation calls for transparency and even vulnerability, as organizational champions communicate needs, weaknesses, and hopes to a global yet decentralized community of innovators. These champions create trust and inspire this innovation community, building enthusiasm through their authenticity and openness and their goal of mutual benefit. And we find that, through this, champions, time and time again, outperform others in all business performance categories.

Champions Drive Operational Optimization

Global organizations are, needless to say, complex, made up of diverse and fragmented teams, processes, and systems. Identifying valuable and relevant resources can be difficult, and therefore most people go with what they know regardless of whether or not it's the best method. Delegation is tough because leaders and employees don't always know who should handle an assignment. Workflow is bottlenecked by policy and politics, duplication of work is enabled by ignorance, and accuracy is often sacrificed for speed or for someone's personal agenda.

For years, quality gurus have helped companies handle organizational and operational challenges through slogans that support policies, such as, "Must comply and conform to agreed-upon requirements." While I support the quality-management concept, I believe its application is much more suited to companies that compete as a commodity—differentiated only by price. If a company sells sand, then by all means, conform to agreed-upon requirements. But as our businesses grow more innovative to meet changing consumer demands, the world becomes less black and white, and more businesses are forced to compete creatively in the gray. Products today are created before consumers even express a need for them. I was perfectly fine, for example, without my car navigation system and DVD player for my kids. But now that I have them, they are requirements. To compete in today's marketplace, we must make room for creativity *and* quality, not just quality. Our operations must support execution *and* imagination, not just execution.

Closing

I was recently in the Chicago airport and walked past several artistic displays. I saw cultural displays featuring communities from around the globe. I saw displays that showed innovation through aviation and how it's opened up worlds of opportunities. I saw a display of the Statue of Liberty made out of Legos holding a modern windmill—representing the importance of our energy-producing times. These displays represented many of the most precious things in life. Surrounding them all was the buzz of progress and hope. As I walked through the terminals, I saw a very capable, driven, and diverse population of people and fell in love with our humanity. I was humbled by our love for the human endeavor.

I love that our humanity leaves room for the progression of the precious things in life, and because of it, we are passionate. I love that in our humanity, we love. I love that we are diverse and brilliant. I love that we value progress and innovation. And I love that we, as a global community, are courageous.

These new and exciting times will demand renewed courage and renewed commitment from leaders. Today, tomorrow, and forever are times for organizational champions—enlightened change makers who are personally committed to mutual values and relentlessly driven by possibilities. They are committed to themselves, to others, and to a worthy mission that they can align with. They are often at the core of successful cultures and behind successful global strategies.

Organizational champions are captivated by the business and social environment today and in the future. It fits them well, though they don't always come out unscathed from it. But no matter how harsh a situation might be, they are consistent in their principles. Their consistency, energy, and curiosity set them up better than others in global organizations.

I hope this journey toward being a champion begins in your life if it hasn't already.

In order to support you in your journey, I invite you into the conversation that is happening around the globe as the organizational champion core principle model continues to be confirmed and understood in application. Please visit www.organizationalchampions.com and participate in the ongoing conversation; give your input and share your stories.

Also, I invite you to contribute to the data being collected behind the core principles of organizational champions by participating in a self-assessment found at www .organizationalchampions.com.

Onward!

ENDNOTES

Chapter 1

1. The World Bank Group, The World Bank GenderStats, 2008, http://web.worldbank.org/WBSITE/EXTERNAL/COUNTRIES/ECAEXT/EXTECAREGTOPGENDER/0,,menuPK:570889~pagePK:51065911~piPK:64171011~theSitePK:570862,00.html, August 2008.
2. "The Enterprise of the Future," IBM Global CEO Study, 2008.
3. SVI Organizational Champions Feedback Survey, August 2008.
4. Dawn Kawamoto and Tom Krazit, "Motorola's Zander Out after Razr Deemed One-Hit Wonder," CNET News, November 2007.

Chapter 2

1. "The Enterprise of the Future," IBM Global CEO Study, 2008.
2. The World Health Organization, *Avian Influenza, 2008*, www.who.int/csr/disease/avian_influenza/en/, June 2008.
3. Steve Bjerklie, "Eco-fat—Tyson Executive Discusses Partnership with ConocoPhillips," *Meat & Poultry*, April 2007.
4. Louis Gerstner, Jr., *Who Says Elephants Can't Dance?* New York: HarperCollins, 2002.

Chapter 3

1. SVI Organizational Champions Feedback Survey, August 2008. Warren G. Bennis and Robert J. Thomas, *Geeks and Geezers: How Era, Values, and Defining Moments Shape Leaders*, Boston: Harvard Business School Press, 2002.
2. "Unlocking the DNA of an Adaptable Workforce," The Global Human Capital Study 2008, New York: IBM Corporation, September 2007.

Chapter 7

1. Graham Wallas, *The Art of Thought*, New York: Harcourt, Brace and Company, 1926.

Chapter 10

1. Jim Collins and Jerry Porras, *Built to Last: Successful Habits of Visionary Companies*, New York: HarperCollins, 1997.
2. Gil Cloyd, "What Is Connect + Develop?" About Connect + Develop Web page on the P&G Connect + Develop Web site, https://secure3.verticali.net/pg-connection-portal/ctx/noauth/0_0_1_4_83_4_3.do.

INDEX

ABOUT THE AUTHOR

Mike Thompson is the founder of SVI, a provider of innovative and highly effective leadership solutions to many of the world's most admired companies, and is a key consultant for Wal-Mart's culture and leadership initiatives. He is often a featured professor for John Brown University's graduate courses in leadership and ethics. Previously, Thomson founded ThompsonMurray, an advertising firm that grew from a two-person start-up to a multi-million-dollar company serving clients such as P&G, Energizer, Michelin, and Coca-Cola.